GREEN-WINGED HORSE

GREEN-WINGED HORSE

New and Selected Poems
By

Lyubomir Levchev

Art Work by
Stoimen Stoilov

New poems translated from Bulgarian by
Valentin Krustev

Editor
Richard Harteis

FIRST EDITION

Little Red Tree Publishing, LLC,
New London, CT. 06320

Copyright © 2013 Lyubomir Levchev

All rights are reserved under International and Pan-American Copyright Conventions. Except for brief passages quoted in a newspaper, magazine, radio or television review, no part of this book may be reproduced in any form or by any means, electronic or mechanical, including photocopying and recording, or by any information storage and retrieval system, without permission in writing from the William Meredith Foundation which has produced this book as the 2013 William Meredith Award for Poetry: www.williammeredithfoundation.org.

First Edition, 2013, manufactured in USA
1 2 3 4 5 6 7 8 9 10 LSI 20 19 18 17 16 15 14 13

Cover and Book Design: Michael John Linnard, MCSD
Book set in: Arial, Times New Roman, Trajan Pro

The digital reproductions of original paintings and drawings by Stoimen Stoilov © are printed here by kind permission, including the front cover. Images appear on pages 58 - 67 [Gallery I], pages 108 - 119 [Gallery II] and pages 194 - 205 [Gallery III].

Photograph of Luybomir Levchev by XingXin Zhang.
Photograph of Stoimen Stoilov reprinted by kind permission.
Photograph of Valentin Krustev reprinted by kind permission.

Poems from *Ashes to Light*, were first published by Curbstone Press and are reprinted by kind permission of Northwestern University Press. Translation copyright © 2013 Valentin Krustev and Jack Harte,

Literal translations in English of the poems from *Sky Break* (Passeggiata Press, 1997), copyright © Chtiliana Halatcheva-Rousseva, appear here as adapted by Niles and Pamela Bond.

Other Previously Published Poems: translation copyright, Valentin Krustev © 2013.

Forewords and introductions, copyright Richard Harteis © 2013.

Library of Congress Cataloging-in-Publication Data (applied for)

Levchev, Lyubomir, April 27, 1935,
 Green-Winged Horse : new and selected poems / by Lyubomir Levchev. -- 1st ed.
  p. cm.
 ISBN 978-1-935656-23-4 (pbk. : alk. paper)
 I. Title. II. Stoimen Stoilov.
 PS3556.I812I25 2013
 811'.54--dc23

Little Red Tree Publishing, LLC,
635 Ocean Avenue,
New London, CT 06320.
website: www.littleredtree.com

The William Meredith Foundation, Inc.
337 Kitemaug Road
Uncasville, Ct. 06382
website: www.williammeredithfoundation.org

CONTENTS

Foreword by Richard Harteis   x
Illustration and title poem: Green-Winged Horse   3

New Poems

A Verbal Portrait   6
Children Gather Autumn Leaves   7
Graffiti   8
Another Threshold   9
Hotel California   10
The Season of the Lonely Cricket   11
The Indian Summer of the Soul   13
The Book   13
The Lover of Solitude   14
In the Invisible Tower   15
The Roman Bridge   15
Ballad for the Tender "No"   16
Funny Nostalgias   17
Tenderness   18
Amnesia   19
Farewell Excitement   20
Shadow   21
Autumn in Salzburg   22
Getting Lost   24
The Frame   25
Occurrence   28
Occurrence with Freckles   29
Parting   30
Seeing   31
Waiting for One's Own Self   32
De Profundis   34
The Spirit is Packing up His Things   35
Above Things   36
Glassy Conditions   37
The Stone Ship   38
Hermeneutics   39
Exhibition   40
It Seems   41
Caprice No. 8   42
Toward Evening   43
Train   43
A Final Talk about Everything   44
Free Sky   45
Infernal Machine   46

Death Galloping on a Pale Horse	47
Mist	48
Foucault's Pendulum	50
Without Tears	52
At Hemingways's House	53
GALLERY I: Art by Stoimen Stoilov	55
Rick Koster: review from *The Day,* New London, CT	56

SKYBREAK: Selected Poems

Foreword by Richard Harteis	72
A Street to Heaven	74
Skybreak	74
Winthrop's Mill	76
So Many Religions	77
Early Morning in New London	77
Clouds	78
Women Waiting for Ships	78
The Sun Ship	79
Night Time or The Golden Saxophone	80
Piano Bar	81
Moonless Calendar	82
Message	85
New London Red	86
Anatomy of Time	88
Winter Rain	89
Spring Is Born	90
Flying Away	91
A Poet in New York	92
Portrait of a City	93
Ruth	94
At the Hideaway Inn	96
Thank You and Goodbye	98
Map of the World	99
The Destruction of Gomorrah	101
GALLERY II: Art by Stoimen Stoilov	103
Window into Time: The Art of Stoimen Stoilov	104

ASHES OF LIGHT: Selected Poems

Review by Zoya Marincheva	122
Gimmebreadye	130

Continuous Poem	132
The Land of the Murdered Poets	133
We Stopped	134
Morning	135
And Here I Am	136
Dénouement	136
Caprice No. 1	137
Caprice No. 2	138
Caprice No. 3	138
Poetry Reading	139
Caprice No. 6	142
Caprice No. 7	143
Caprice No. 11	144
The Garden Before Paradise	145
Letter	147
Love in the Military Hospital	148
I Who Did Not Flee Pompeii	150
Tomorrow's Bread	151
Lighthouse	153
Pier	155
Caprice No. 16	156
The Universe Is and Anonymous Creator	157
The Bottles	158
The Last Caprice	160
Path	161
The Gardens of Eternity	162
A Double Ballad	164
Ridge	165
The Wall	166
The Cat Is Drinking Water from My Glass	168
Not Far from the Shore	170
Semantic Seeds	171
A Tale from Twenty-Four Thousand, Four Hundred and Fifty-One Nights	173
Ultima Verba	176
The Stone	178
Ashes of Light	180
Distance XXI	182
Irish Fantasies	183
Lullaby	186
SMS	187
Insomnia	188
Night Knife	189
Spiderman	190
Fall	192

GALLERY III: Art by Stoimen Stoilov 193

Other Previously Published Poems

A Song to Garcia Lorca	208
A Song about Lightning Rods	209
Appassionato	210
Tango	210
Positions	211
My Mother in Paradise	211
Daytime Moon	213
Soul	213
Poem	215
Carmen	216
After Finishing the Cognac	217
The Good Samaritan	218
Gunshot	219
Pose 13	220
Cockfight	222
The Bells of Isla Negra	223
Image	224
Adventure	224
A Curse on Columbus	225
Afterlove	227
Christmas	227
Saint Victory	230
Caprice No. 18	231
Roofs	231
The Deceptive Play of the Seasons (New London Quartet)	233
1. Spring Viola	233
2. Summer Violin	233
3. Autumn Cello	234
4. And Winter Clavichord	235
Translator: Valentin Krustev	237
Artist: Stoimen Stoilov	238
About the Author: Lyubomir Levchev	240

FOREWORD

The William Meredith Foundation, in co-operation with the Griffis Art Center, Little Red Tree Publishing, and private sponsors is honored to present the 2013 William Meredith Award for Poetry to Bulgarian poet, Lyubomir Levchev. The Meredith Award for poetry has no application process, but comes to the author unsolicited in the spirit of generosity that informed Meredith's interaction with the world of poetry when he judged competitions and invited poets to the Library of Congress as US Poet Laureate. The William Meredith Award for Poetry helps preserve the legacy of an extraordinary human being and the impact he has had on so many lives. Poet, pilot, arborist, beloved teacher and friend, this legacy is a treasure we wish to guarantee for future generations.

As First Lady Hillary Rodham Clinton noted in a letter celebrating Meredith's 80th birthday, "The arts have always been a unifying force in our world, bringing people together across vast cultural, social, economic and geographical divisions. Through his work, William Meredith both enhances and strengthens the American spirit. As you honor Mr. Meredith, you celebrate the timeless power of poetry and poets as our American memory, our purveyors of insight and culture, our eyes and ears who silence the white noise around us, and express the very heart of what connects us, plagues us, and makes us fully human."

In 2009, the Hygienic Art Gallery opened a fine exhibition tracing the history of years of friendship between the artistic communities in Bulgaria and the city of New London. The bridge between our countries first took form when William served as the Poet Laureate of the US and invited Lyubomir Levchev and other Bulgarian poets to the Library of Congress in 1980. An ardent Cultural Attaché from the Bulgarian Embassy, Krassin Himmirski lobbied hard for Bulgarian poetry and explained the renaissance in this art form that was taking place in Bulgaria at the time, preparing the way for these invited poets. In the following years, William visited Bulgaria many times and helped establish scholarships, art exhibits, readings and publications, and for this work in the culture he was accorded Bulgarian citizenship by presidential decree in 1996. Meredith always defended democratic values and artistic freedom during those sometimes contentious writers' symposia in Sofia, but he always maintained that if poets can not meet and know each other at the human level, to shake hands across political borders as it were, there is no hope for any progress. And so his friendship with Lyubomir Levchev and his family and other Bulgarian artists deepened. He continued to support the wonderful artist exchanges and projects that began to take form through the generosity of the Griffis Art Center in co-operation with Lyubomir Levchev's own Orpheus Foundation. And so, this award recognizes not only Levchev's talent as a poet, but also the brotherhood in the art each man felt for the other.

There is an oft quoted proverb that success has many fathers, while failure is an orphan. Fortunately for New London and Bulgaria, the extraordinary relationship that was born between the artistic communities of our two countries in the 90's has now fully matured and continues to grow through succeeding progeny. It stands as a remarkable achievement, a model of how artists can grow and prosper and help us in our common human endeavor when good will, hard work, philanthropy and talent come together.

While Levchev's poems sometimes obliquely take on political positions — how could they not, politics is, after all, simply the way people live and organize their lives in society—the publication of this book recognizes his talent as a poet, not as a politician. In his memoir, *You Are Next*, published in English in the US and in Bulgaria, he addresses the question quite candidly himself, refusing to recant a lifetime dedicated to socialist ideals while recognizing the failures of Communism.

The Russian critic Maxim Zamshev gives us this rather subtle analysis: "Levchev matured as a poet in the 1970's and the 1980's. The surrounding world was also changing. Good and evil were continuing their fight even under peaceful conditions, and sometimes that fight was no less furious than the fight on the real battle fields. The poet has preserved throughout the years his understanding that the poet's force is in his ability to endure, to keep silent, to lead the readers along the serpentine paths of his poems, in the ability to turn the temporary failure into a constant victory. Man has no right to lose: this is the figurative quintessence of Levchev's poetry of the seventies and eighties."

As noted in the introduction to *Skybreak*, Levchev's career represents a "lifetime of verbal mastery and careful observation. His speech is informed by a metaphorical vision of great beauty and power. It is a unique voice, that of a poet, like his native Bulgaria, caught between past and future, East and West, who ultimately transcends these polarities. At various times sad, bemused, giddy, mystified, awestruck, and wise, it is often a lonely voice; and when there is no audience, he is content to sing to the stars. Like Shelley or other great Romantics, he speaks to us directly, a lyrical leap out of space and time. In the East it is said that 'between one person and another there is only light.' The world is brighter for the light that shines in this work."

The inclusion of Stoimen Stoilov's art in this volume continues what is becoming a tradition for Little Red Tree in publishing a healthy collection of visual art to balance its poetry. Despite what some purists may believe - that poems should stand alone, naked on the blank page - Little Red Tree sees no contradiction in having these two art forms speak to each other in a book. Such art is not meant to "illustrate" but enhance the work Michael Linnard is publishing so beautifully these days. Not only are Stoimen and Luybomir longstanding friends, but each of them knew and loved William Meredith. Stoilov's generosity knew no bounds when it came to providing art for publications. His marvelous illustrations of Meredith's poem eulogizing the loss of 128 sailors on the SS Thresher were presented to all the families of those lost at sea. His work graces many volumes of poetry published in the US and he has exhibited his work widely in the US. Two reviews of his work precede the paintings found in the galleries here, as do reviews of the volumes selected for inclusion with the newly translated poems.

In *Window on the Black Sea*, we felt it necessary to say a word about translation and, so it is here. When we asked poet friends to consider translating for that volume, one poet in particular said she could not use the time remaining to her in life this way, that all one could say about an interesting translation was that it must have been beautiful in the original. And its true that in a sense, all translations are adaptations. This is the case here as well, depending on who has translated the work, some being more or less literal translations, others such as those in *Skybreak* reworked by Niles and Pamela Bond as adaptations. William Meredith's masterful translation of Levchev's poem "Roofs" is an example of how politics and personal anecdote may blend seamlessly while adding a rhyme scheme not found in the original poem. But the fingerprints of so many translators can be found on so many of the poems, it is sometimes impossible to assign credit to one translator or another. *Green-Winged Horse* features a great number of new poems, however, uniquely translated by Valentin Krustev. Here once again, history and talent come together in friendly synchronicity. Valentin was one of William's oldest friends, and was one of the very first translators assigned to William when he first began attending Peace the Hope of the Planet, the writers conferences sponsored by the Union of Bulgarian Writers over the decades. Valentin's friendship has been essential in the voluminous correspondence and translations required over the years to keep projects on target. He has our deep and abiding gratitude for the hard work and professionalism he always exhibited.

After an extended visit to New London sponsored by the Griffis Art Center, under the enlightened hospitality of its director, Sharon Griffis, Lyubomir wrote a beautiful series of poems, *Skybreak*, in which he dedicates poems to all his new friends in America. In the title poem he writes,

> "William has reigned over many a
> chasm. And he presented this chasm to me:
> New England - The secret garden of poets."

The gift we have all received in return has been the friendship of so many extraordinary Bulgarian artists, and the chance to share our work and our lives with each other because of the generosity of the Griffis Art Center and the Orpheus Foundation. It's in the shelter of each other that we live, the Irish say. The story of these friendships gives heart, and recalls the opening lines from William's poem, "Dalhousie Farm:"

> "Will you live long enough to sit in the shade
> Of that tree, old man? the children asked,
> And the old Chinaman planting the sapling replied,
> This world was not a desert when I came into it.
> Now, I myself have raised some thrifty trees
> And children, entirely from words,
> But it is friends with real trees and children who will become,
> Probably, my testimony, my best tongue."

Richard Harteis
President
WilliamMeredithFoundation.org
Paris, May 2013

ACKNOWLEDGEMENTS

The William Meredith Foundation wishes to acknowledge with deep gratitude the following organizations and sponsors whose financial and moral support have made the awarding of this publication possible.

Little Red Tree Publishing
The Griffis Arts Center
John and Loraine Hracyk
Evelyn Prettyman

THE GREEN-WINGED HORSE

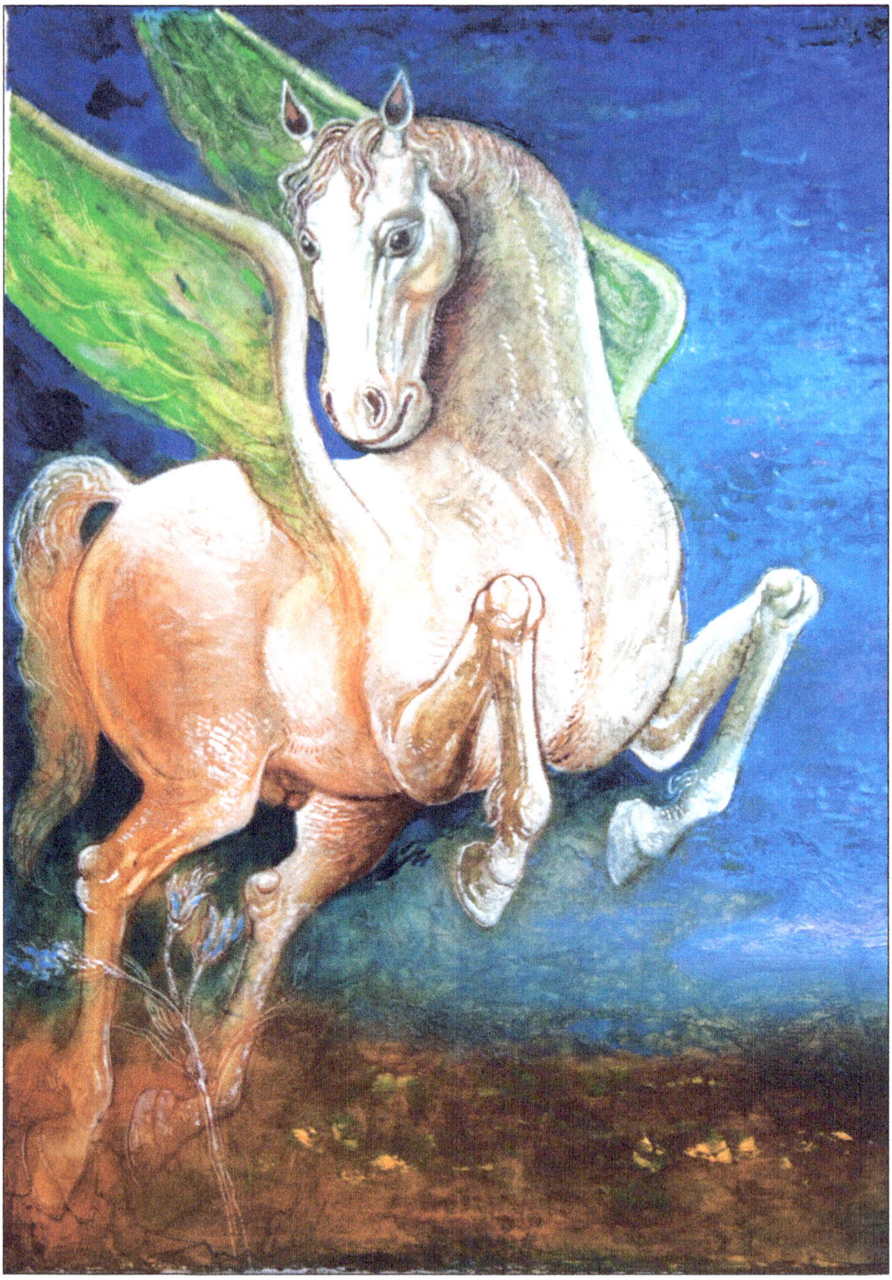

GREEN-WINGED HORSE

In spring everything flourishes.
Not only flowers and blossoms,
but buds and leaves too.
Even invisible things flourish,
but they are very fragile.

Little branch, broken by the wind.
Little branch, with two buds and three leaves,
I wanted to pick you up from the road
where you had fallen, before some truck

crushed you, but I was afraid
they might say that I had broken you.

I... What a mean coward I was.

I walk toward my end without fear,
and I feel you dip into my heart
as if into an antique vase, and
I sense how beautiful you are.

Little branch, when I fade
into the distance, when
I become quite little,
you'll become my little horse.

You'll be my green-winged horse.

New Poems

A VERBAL PORTRAIT

Calm down! It's not
the end of the world.

My friend, the American artist
Mark McKee has painted me
on a piece of wood thrown ashore
by the tide after shipwreck. And I
feel as if I've been served a summons.

Connecticut, Mystic Seaport,
a shore where the shadow
of my soul is still roaming
while I am on the yonder shore.

I am standing like a hieroglyph
with outstretched arm.

I am being introduced to myself:
"Nice to meet you!"

It's me, of course, with this
furrow between the eyebrows,
and this third eye. I am a sketch
done from memory. I am a
verbal portrait. But who is
hunting me? And why?
The question repeats me.

If hope has lost me
tell her that I don't lose hope.
In case the arrow is searching for love,
show it where my heart abides.

Look! My smile is swimming
in the Ninth Wave's sea.

White clouds like paramedics
bend their heads over me.
They're saying something softly.
They don't want me to hear them.
But I make out
what the anchor's chain
and the ship's bell
tell each other:

"It's all coming to an end,"
they say. Everything has an end.

Ships also die, like people.
Only two things,
the universe and love,
end without end.

CHILDREN GATHER AUTUMN LEAVES

This show has
many acts and scenes.

Act one:
Autumn gathers children
in the city parks.

Then:
Children gather autumn leaves.
With enthusiastic cries
they foretell leaps and flights
or say prayers to some deity of theirs.

Children gather autumn leaves—
not in their hands, but in open arms,
and they hide something sacred in their hearts.
Is that a lesson? Or a game? Or magic?
The teachers hide behind the trees
in case they break off someone's wings.

Children gather autumn leaves.
Or perhaps it's vice versa.
Maybe one should say that
the leaves gather children's voices.
And the fair season leaves.
And in the invisible house of this universe,
the beginning and the end embrace each other.

GRAFFITI

Time is not one.
But, once upon a time
there was a time when
the future was seen best
from the top of barricades.
Where to find paving stones now?
The streets of Paris have long been
covered with asphalt…

Once upon a time
there was a banner
with three words
and three hearts.
The sky unfurled it.
The wind extolled it.
They who were about to die,
kissed it. But meanwhile,
Fear betrayed Liberty.
Avarice destroyed Equality.
Envy killed Brotherhood.

Just a pole remained then
from the banner, like the
skeleton of a scarecrow,
like frozen lightning.

Meanwhile, urchins scribble on the walls:
We need a new dream!
We need a new mast from whose
crow's nest to see a New World.

ANOTHER THRESHOLD

I am sitting on the threshold.
There, where the lonely past
once sat, staring at the horizon,
as if waiting for me. Now
I am here. The horizon
watches me. And I think:
How many vistas does this threshold have?
One of them is the road
that has led me here.
The other is the door
that will open one day
and lead me where it should.
The third one…
A light breeze rises.
It leafs the pages of today's newspaper,
and reads to me aloud
flighty news, seeds of hatred,
from which no history sprouts.
Meanwhile, I count the strikes
of the village church bell.
Later on, I count sheep.
And I fall asleep.
But I already know that
honeybees are dying worldwide.
They say it's due to our cell phones,
PCs and the like, "smart machines"
that irradiate us fatally.
And the little bees lose the ability
to find their native hive,
the honeycomb –
the little cell of meaning.
And what remains
is just the golden humming,
the symbol, the metaphor, the
awful simile for our mutual fate.
Like them, I'm also trying to escape
the bad dream, Doomsday…

But there is still some time left
before the door opens, isn't there?
I open my eyes. I am sitting on
some other threshold.
And what is creeping this way
is not a fog.
Fallen clouds
come and lick my hand.

HOTEL CALIFORNIA

To my son

I'm driving slowly
along the night road.
Not because I don't know it.
On the contrary,
I remember it's perilous turns.

I'm driving slowly
because my soul likes dangers,
but it doesn't like turns.

Slowly, the headlights
shove through big,
winged trees –
guardian angels,
bending over me.
And suddenly they
or someone else,
afraid that I may fall asleep,
turn on some music.
Jericho trumpets echo.
They tear down my walls.
How do they know that I like
"Hotel California?"
But can I hire a room in a song?
It is too late to ask
a bell gone silent,
a candle extinguished.
The guitars have already
confessed their sins.
The car has stopped by force of habit
at the fountain I used to call ours.
The moon horse is
drinking water
from the stone trough.

The universe smells of pine and resin—
a drug for ghosts and witches.
It is dangerous to search for the meaning
of this world: bodily passions,
a temple of a soul undone.
That yellow light in the distance
is the entrance to a merry nursing home.

There they make final love,
call one another best friends,
and drink 1935 vintage wine.

I drink strong water
from my fountain
and splash my face to be sure
it hasn't run away by chance.
No Beast, no She, no Captain
can forbid me. This maze is mine.
It has many exits, but
has no entrance anymore.

THE SEASON OF THE LONELY CRICKET

For Elka Nyagolova

Solitude. Only you, only I.
Like a city cricket
my inner voice asks itself:

Why are horizons frittered away?
Is this a taking off or a return?
Shots dying away or lightning
waking up? The crunching sound of
snarling doors?

Or history is feeding
on poisonous tall tales?
And that is why it goes mad so often.
As well as we alongside it.

Metaphors! What kind of weakness
is it to compare sentimental thoughts
with thoughtful feelings?...
We imagine that we invent them,
while they dream of being
understood by us....

77 bewitched doors! I open them.
I go into deserted spaces. A home,
a fortress, or a temple,
now it's all the same,
once even my faithful dog
failed to recognize me.
In Ithaca, they are not
waiting for anybody anymore.

Only a forgotten radio is
playing Antonio Vivaldi's seasons.

"Are there still four,"
the lonely little cricket asks,
pretending to be communicating
with God. "Isn't what I'm playing
the fifth season?"

Isn't our Earth itself
a sort of a radio
left playing in the Universe?
Lonely, matchless, wasted.
Yet, someone has turned it on
and left. "Could it have been me,
Lord," my sidekick asks.

Then he turns abruptly
towards some hidden force,
towards some mysterious
reason and portending star:
"Whoever you are,
stop hiding yourself!
I've come for you:
to hug you for the last time
and to waste myself in you.

Hatred failed to kill me.
Who knows, love may succeed."

THE INDIAN SUMMER OF THE SOUL

The blackbirds are picking up apples for me.
The angels are picking up words for me.
So, it seems as if I'm not doing anything.
It seems as if last night
I left my heart in
a love at last sight.
But where was that?
I remember how I came out of myself.
I remember how in the park
someone was playing an amorous waltz
for his empty hat.
Then…
I'm thinking…
But can one think after that?

THE BOOK

The words think that I have gone to sleep.
The book falls out of my hand the way
a bird falls from a spellbound branch.
But it doesn't fall on the floor,
careful not to crush the shadows,
or on the sky, careful not
to make the stars crumble.

And I am not reading
all that anymore.
I am just watching
how a book drops
from the hands of some
overly tired humanity,
and remains floating—
an cosmonaut in weightlessness
singing of some Motherland...
But she hears and knows.

Then you, darling, reach out
from the other side of things
and undermine the meaning whispering:
"Do you want something else?

Another half-darkness?
Another half-sleep?
Another… book?"

Yes, I do, of course!
But what is a book without love?
People want love.
Not half, but all of it.
Even if it is sad.
Even if it is hopeless.
People want love.
So do I.
I want to read it.
I want to read you
to the end.

THE LOVER OF SOLITUDE

A change is taking place in the world.
The dangerous seeker of meaning
already feels the dream has begun to go blind.
Nearby things are easier to see;
The more remote ones fade in the distance.
They vanish slowly like embittered angels,
like horizons that have lost their faith.

All right. I accept the truth in cold blood.
Nearby things don't need dreamers.
All they need is an outstretched hand.

Look, the remote control
changes the channel.
Boring ads are filling you up
as if you were a fridge.
The news report keeps repeating
what it wants to come true
And it depersonalizes you.

"Who are you?"
nearby things ask.
And, unwillingly,
I give myself away.
"I am the lover of aloneness."

IN THE INVISIBLE TOWER

Last night it rained gold.
It still smells of God.

Autumn's bedding,
tumbled by passion, lies deserted.

The women look at one another, glowing.
But not knowing which one is Danaë.

THE ROMAN BRIDGE

For Ivan Marazov

The road has sunk into the mountain.
The empire has collapsed into traditions.
The age has drained away into a mystic pothole.
Only you, Roman bridge, are whole,
a purposeless survivor.
Bridge of passion.
Bridge of vengeance.
Bridge of rapture…

What do you want, Rhodope monster?
Where are you leading to, hunchbacked show?
Nothing flows under you anymore.
You don't have either end anymore.

You are endless.
I wonder what you connect
if you too can't make both ends
meet anymore? Why do I like you?
Perhaps because my madness and
yours are both the same.
Above you, a lonely little cloud goes by,
like the soul of a forgotten God.

But, in fact, in reality,
to whom am I speaking?

BALLAD FOR THE TENDER "NO"

I sit invisible
on the bench behind the bush.
And for no apparent reason
the rain turns into snow,
and you turn into a memory.

I watch you trying
to live without me,
and I see how I fail
living without you.

No. No. No.
I am now sufficiently impossible.
I saw the heart of history meet
secretly with the history of heart.

What does doomed mean?

No. No.
Those are just internal visions,
bullet sacraments.

In a forest of dead words
we seek our souls.
Instead of leaves,
prayer showers from the arid sky.

Please, whisper that ban to me again,
so I can infringe upon it again
like the thief, who returns in you
through an unlocked
tender "No".

FUNNY NOSTALGIAS

I grieve secretly
for the age when
time was measured
in poured out sand
or water, or fire.

Space was measured in time.
From here to the sacred source of things
is three hours on horseback.
And after another race, just as long,
you'll face a sunset,

and everything is visible.

I grieve secretly
for the age when
letters and numbers
used to be written
with the same symbols.

How much more mystery there was in them!

Since we are trying to be precise,
what happened exactly? I don't know.
Maybe knowledge overcame wisdom.
Quantity overcame quality.
Pleasure overcame happiness.
Shamelessness overcame conscience.
Permissiveness, this Dostoyevsky's nightmare,
overcame freedom.

Sooner or later, those victories
will be vanquished too.
But humanity, I pray and hope
that it's not too late for you at least.

As for me, for the future, I'll maintain
these ridiculous nostalgias.

TENDERNESS

Everything is like you.
Time hurts, like you.
I am afraid to tell you,
but time is changing, like you.

Perhaps you miss the children,
the looking after them,
bringing them to reason.
Yes, they are gone. Only
love and anxiety remain,
while the cause is gone.
But, whom are you talking with?
The reason for it all, right?

You are scolding that little cloud:

"Watch out! You're little, you'll fall.
And you'll turn into fog and frost."
You are also angry at the forest stream:
"You've been wading in the river again.
You're icy cold! Get out in the sun, right away!"

Take it easy, darling!
They are like me.
They too are afraid of telling you
that time is changing.
And you have turned into a child
playing a strict mother
in the theater of our shadows.

But what can I do,
once I have forgotten my part?
And all I can remember is the tenderness.

AMNESIA

The world looks
as clear as autumn.
And in this clarity
I wait to see
what else lies
in store for me.

But I don't see. Instead, I hear
the world cuckoo calling.
A cuckoo? And what does it foretell?
A crisis, of course. A world crisis!
All right, then. Find it a strait jacket.

We have forgotten the language of birds.
We have forgotten
that the first God was a bird.

We have forgotten
that the soul lives in the branches of memory,
not in the machine for forgetting.

Why don't you say something, machine-operators?
Yes, it can be heard.
Some kind of knocking.
A woodpecker?
Another God?
A clock?
A blind man's little walking stick?

Is time really blind?

Today, all ideals have turned into icons
with gouged out eyes.
So that is why we don't see,
but only hear…

I agree to be a dog,
a guide for blind times.

FAREWELL EXCITEMENT

If there were really a beginning,
in the beginning, as in a hallucination,
I'd hear Sir Andrew Lloyd Webber's cats.
I wouldn't say that I'm his greatest fan.

But they, they sang and woke me tenderly.
The wind had ruffled the ridiculous curtain of the window
making it possible to see the passing of
the fishmonger, an old sailor, now just a fisherman,
a smuggler of street illusions.

All his transformations
had left their imprint on his face:
a face the color of an ancient amphora,
a face overgrown with seaweed,
a face drawn out from the evening trawl…

Since the clue is dark,
and this dark lane is steep,
the face would be pushing the bike.
And the fish bag with the living catch
is quivering with farewell excitement.
Excitement! That's the key word.

Meanwhile, Sir Andrew Lloyd Webber's cats
follow the wheel of the history ending
like an escort, like a ceremonial corps de ballet…

Those sorts of cats don't like bank clerks
writing poems. Those cats know
that at the end the fisherman will
throw them a little fish,
but a golden one.
And they sing to it.

The first woman shows up,
in a hurriedly thrown on bathrobe
her hair the golden crown.
Above her: the first rays of sun,
the rays showing everything.
The tender female fingers
choose a live fish:
what divine eroticism!

Meanwhile, the old fisherman takes out a cigarette,
bites off the filter, spits it out and lights up…

The sun arrives gallantly
above the roofs like a warm
bosom. The flame explodes.

My world burns to ashes.

SHADOW

For Nickolay Maistorov

I heard the creaking of the invisible staircase.
I heard the howl of dogs gone wild.
And once again I thought:
Something dangerous is making its way into reality.

Then the tender earthquakes began to rock me
as if lulling a stolen child to sleep.

In the beginning, as well as at the end,
was chaos. All testimonies
vanished. All friendships disappeared
I remained alone to drink
my madness to the bottom.
Alone among the bar's
glassy chattering teeth,
Finally, I growled at my silhouette:
"Well, come on, get up!
It's time for us to go as well!..."

And suddenly I realized that somebody
had stolen my shadow, leaving
his instead.

Yes! That was another shadow.
It smelled of a cave.
And it clung to me like a bat.
I left it drag me where it wished,
and suck out meaning and purpose.

It took me home. Good. Thanks.
Be off with you now. And for good.
I love my shadow. And you
are someone else's, whore.
I'd lain down in my clothes,
but, half asleep, I felt her
covering me gently with the blanket.
"What the hell do you want?
Don't you understand that
they have swapped us?"

"No!" She said. "No! I am yours.
It wasn't I that was changed,
but the light.
The source of the world was changed.
Time's direction was changed.

And now it will be even harder to tell
people from their shadows. until everything
becomes personal and multiple,
global and solitary…"
But, I think that…
It's not to be!

AUTUMN IN SALZBURG

For Marta and Yanna

The modern building in the ancient city
is shining like a premature thought,
(as it did with Leonardo).

Through the glass balcony
in the modern building
the ancient wind
and the ancient sun
enter timelessly.

They enter the way a loving grandpa
and grandma, who have come to visit
the beloved grandchildren,
look around furtively.

But in the modern building
there's not a soul—
offspring create future.

The ancient wind
leafs through the last book
of the Gutenberg era
and discerns nothing.
The ancient sun moves ray by ray
and takes a look at the
secluded rooms with crystal walls.
Yes, everything is transparent,
but nothing can be seen.
Only modern sounds
waft freely. Bach is easily
jazzed up, Beethoven's
a harder nut to crack.

Doesn't the modern universe
remind you of the crucible
or the retort of an alchemist?
Albert the Great failed to
solve the mystery.
Are they experimenting again
to turn us into something else?

In ancient Salzburg
I saw one of Mozart's harpsichords.
Its black keys were white,
the white ones were black.

Dusk came sifting down from the castle.
And autumn, without a crucible
or incantations, was turning
broad-leaved plants into
blood-stained gold.

GETTING LOST

If you decide to get lost,
do it in Paris, but be sure
that it's at night. Then
the Métro is closed,
the buses are asleep, and
even the cabs are snoozing
with one headlight on.
But there are ghosts.
Mainly the ghosts of women.
Some of them beautiful.
some even Bulgarian.
Ask them what you like,
except one thing, their age.

Oh! With time and ghosts you
don't talk about time and ghosts.
This is the stuff of politicians.

The last time I got lost,
I was walking through these same
boulevards with unfamiliar names.
I had already seen all this.

I was walking among memories,
which, just like me, had gotten lost
in the green-and-violet rain.
They too believed they remembered
everything, but likewise
didn't know where they were.

Where is the road going to,
if there is a road?
There is, of course!
Once I've said: "For one last time,"
along my way, there is.
And maybe there, right there,
is that impenetrable place, where
you cease to know where you are.

THE FRAME

For Vladimir and Boyan

1.

Wars of worlds!
Ferocities befitting
the untalented Thersites!
Star Wars! Junkie visions!
Oh, God! Would that one
never looked at the sky!

And once those fireflies above were mine.

Yes, once, and there have always been wars.
I became an orphan in a *world* one.
I became a father in a *cold* one.
I am going to die in an infinite, *secret* one.
Meanwhile, the surrogates of man
are assembling the global doom.

That is the frame called life.

I try to put in it
an artificial smile.
I try to become virtual.
But the result is primary twilight.

If it were at least a dream,
I would have managed to find
an oracle to interpret me.

2.

In what's left of reality
the Old Woman and I are
climbing up the marble cloud.
John Donne! John Donne!—
a tired bell is tolling.
An invisible plane flies over.
But don't ask questions.
Not everything has to be clear.
Clarity has no stairway.
And the cloud will fall apart.

Well, that's enough!
This is the ceiling of the world,
the Old Woman says.

Look there, at the end there are
abandoned square orioles.
Of all the images,
of the proud mind,
of fame and vanity,
only those dusty frames remain
dreaming of second use.

Take whatever frame you are looking for.
Pay. And go away.

   3.

Naive doctor,
Dad, you, who used to bandage
wanted rebels, instead of healing
yourself, I seek you feverishly!
As if you have sent me to buy
you a newspaper, and have got
lost in the news about new larcenies
and murders, about new generations
of missiles. I desperately seek you
in what I think you sought.
I search for you in the sad eyes
of the plain illusions, still waiting
in front of your doctor's office.
I search for you in their silence.

I search for you at the springs
of St. Barbara, where a malarial sun
is still taking leave of the tobacco warehouses.
A woman springs up from a forgotten island.
A black dog muzzled by a green
full moon, is running after her…
 Shouldering the frame,
my wounded border,
I choose even shadier sidewalks,
I become even more obscure…

Suddenly a street lamp
will entrap me. And will blind me.
And I will crash into myself.

4.

My father hurries. He has
received a call from someone sick…
I have called him.
But I am ashamed to admit it.

My father is younger than me.
Younger than my son.
Younger than my wound.

He smiles at me:
Where are you headed with this frame?
You look like a walking doorframe to me,
the aura of a creature, which has existed
before us, a rainbow, the flash of a thought …

I am on my way to you, father.
The world has become a
difficult place to live in,
a hiding place crammed with memories.
The epochs pass, but their
unbearableness remains.
Look how many generations are jostling
each other like doors during an earthquake.
I wish at least one of them was an exit.

And I pray to you:
Our Father, let me play a little
outside life, outside the frame.
And help me open the outward door.
Once you lent me the beginning,
lend me also the end!

OCCURRENCE

I met a Man from another world.
He was examining the traffic lights.
"That's you, right?"
He nods.
"I have long wanted to ask you something.
I have seen so many times
'The Secret Supper'
or 'The Last…'.
You know best.
But I…
Why can't I tell
who of them is Judas?
All are thoughtful,
anxious.
handsome in some way…
But who of them is Judas?"
The man smiles condescendingly:
"No one can tell
before one is kissed."
"I've been kissed so many times!..."
"Oh, do you remember?"
"Yes, sometimes… Or suddenly."
"Well, that's the rising from the dead
that no one believes in.
You remember!
What more do you want?"

OCCURRENCE WITH FRECKLES

The cars stop at the traffic lights.
The rain doesn't stop at the traffic lights.

Having pierced the cloud
the sun shines in my eyes.
I turn sideways. And…
Wow, what a babe
in the car by my side!
What soft freckles!
Two hand spans separate us
(nervy nearness)
but also two wet
windows with goggle-eyed raindrops.
Now, probably I too look goggle-eyed.
The babe is mad
and pulls the car forward.
So do I.
Now she is laughing.
But the magic,
ah, the magic doesn't start.
The magic's gone.
It always goes that way.
Moreover, those weren't freckles,
but just shadows,
slender shadows of raindrops.

PARTING

"And out you set for some far off place.
And you'll get there some time or other."
—Alexander Gerov

It's no use sniffing the air, my friend.
Everything smells of departure.
The door upwards is left open.
You liked to run off, didn't you?
I'll close my eyes. But how it hurts!
It's already intolerable!
This passing is part of my long,
long, long euthanasia.

First, you must kill
the damned imagination.
Then, the forces guarding you.
Run, my friend! Run!
You were the only soul
that recognized me in the dark.
Do the same there, in the hereafter,
in the so called Ithaca.
Gods forbid to be recognized after death.
But you yourself used to be the God
of exactly that kingdom
and you have resigned yourself.
Keep in mind my request.

There, amidst the feast of oblivion,
I want you to lick my hand.
Have no pain. Have no fear.

The rest is Telemachus' job.

SEEING

"There is a word vested in death."
—Jesus Navin

I see clearly how the future
and the past mix together.
If you pour calmly,
the two liquids keep their parti-
colored layers for a long time
It is beautiful. But always
someone shakes the cup
that won't pass you by.

I see clearly that
Providence abides in Providence.

"Nonsense!"the attending say,
dressed in new suits.
You are absolutely off your rocker.
Don't confuse Slavic with
Anglo-Saxon wording.
The result will be a
horrible arbitrariness.
Do you remember how at one point,
some new Kremlin visionary
decided to produce a new cocktail.
which he dubbed, as I recall,
"A Soyuz – Apollo," the apotheosis
of peaceful coexistence.
Vodka + Bourbon, fifty/fifty.
So what? The result was still
a Molotov cocktail. Again a blast.
Again blood. Again why…

Because again we had not agreed
who's the future, who's the past.

Again or not, I clearly see that
Providence abides in Providence –
A city and a port in Rhode Island,
north from New London, where
at the end of the 20th century
a cocktail of unhappiness and

happiness, of faith and despair,
of premises and endings
made me a clairvoyant.
And here I am, watching how
I'm pouring into myself just
one transparent liquid
of slow hours and rapid years.
And now no one can shake me.

Hiding a mountain in my heart,
I walk across the valleys,
solitary, as far as I go.

And then the words get dressed up.

WAITING FOR ONE'S OWN SELF

Predatory technologies take thought
away from a brain deprived of faith.
The senses have lost confidence.
The obvious has become dubious.
Only feelings still make use
of antiquated rules.

Down lies the coast.
Up, begins infinity.

Down is the port
where nothing new landed today.
Up – the church
in which for quite some time
even God hasn't entered.
And yet, still yet again
at this idle moment the bells
begin a conversation with
the hoarse ship's whistles.
The sound gives rise to the sign,
the letter, the brand, the mark,
the trace of time's footprint.

And the residual quiet
does not wish to reign.
Is not a calm before the storm.
Is no hindrance.
It even helps me
to hear the whisper of
two neighboring mail-boxes.
Their tin lips curse
the electronic pandemic.

This virtuality depopulates us.
Solitude immobilizes us.
Something has to happen,
to emerge, to explode.

And then I decide that I have
waited long enough for my self.
Well forgotten, I am returning
to the impossible small town of whalemen.
They have a dream of a boat full of the future.
But instead, a stranger turns up.
He is coming from the port.
He goes into the church.
He is bringing thirst,
courage and beginning.

His free manner has
pierced the dream like a
harpoon, like a question:
"Did you lose all that?
Was it you, who forgot
what I found on the
point of the harpoon?"

DE PROFUNDIS

Here I am, at last.
At home.
As difficult as in oneself.
A maze of books.
A double bed.
However, is that the tender fortress?
At the hour of old ivory
I'm listening to your breathing.
Quiet –
like all important things.
Incomprehensible –
like a doctor's handwriting.
A whisper of the soul
run away from the words
that hold everything
I can be envied for,
that is, everything.
I'm listening to your breathing—
and I'm feeling like a thief inside the temple.
Do Gods breathe?
I have never asked myself this question.
He, who was interrogating me,
liked to say:
Never ask a question
that you don't have at least two answers to.
History is clumsy.
Lyrics – silly.
And I don't dare to caress you.

Out of the depths of the Basilica di San Clemente –
deeper
than the tomb of Constantine Cyril the Philosopher,
deeper
than the martyrs' catacombs,
deeper
than the Etruscans' hiding places—
from the deep
an echo can be heard,
an echo of something that is flowing out
and makes me kneel.
Rome, forgive me for the rhymes,
for the barbarian manner
in which I loved you,
and set you on fire…
Here I am at last…

I don't dare…
I'm about to be done...
Lest this sheet,
which is crackling
as if secret answers flow through it,
should wake you up.
I listen to your breathing,
therefore I exist.
God, if you don't believe,
look downwards!
Inwards!
At the end...
The end of the universe,
Steven Hawking claims,
is not an edge of an abyss.
Therefore, we won't sink tracelessly.

THE SPIRIT IS PACKING UP HIS THINGS

For Tosho Toshev

Memory is the house of the soul.
Casual words. How come, you have
remembered them, my friend?
The door stands open.
Inside it is quite untidy.
The spider is swinging:
he fancies that he is the
pendulum of loneliness.
"Listen, guy, right here
I had hidden my notebook
with secrets." Damn it!
Who's been rummaging here?
The spider makes a sign for me to get closer.
When I bend down,
he shoots a whisper into me:
"Your spirit is packing up his things…"
"What do you mean?"
"I mean that he is packing up his things."

Silence. Everything's forgotten.
O, God, what a wonderful thing
silence is, in which souls go and come,
talking about the Angel Michael.

ABOVE THINGS

Well, let's go on playing.

Down – everything flows past.
Up – everything flies off.
And you, entering the halls of light,
are looking at the cloudy conditions
murmuring: – They look like snowmen.
White giants licking cotton candy.

Did you hear that mankind
is getting on in years? Snowmen
too live increasingly longer.
Children grow up ever faster.
They mature in all respects.
They get disappointed.
They emigrate into timelessness, and
the snowmen have to wait for them
longer and longer. They turn into
snow dwarfs, sick of spring,
with coal eyes gone blind,
with carrot noses pecked out,
hunchback gnomes brooming
a way for the global modernity.

Wait, this looks like a self-portrait.

I've never liked tales of
giants and dwarfs,
or of run away children,
deprived of paths
and the global warming.
But, in the end, in order
to have something flowing,
something should be melting.
And in order to have things that
fly off, be above things.

When my mom had no money to buy me skates,
she would say: "Be above things.
Come, let's make a snowman, or a cloudman.
All right, mom, all right.
All that has happened.
Look, I am the cloudman.
But where are those unhappy things?

Strange rays fall.
The airplane descends for landing.
Everything feels heavy.
Everything strives for the earth.

Except the soul.

GLASSY CONDITIONS

A bird crashed into me and I realized,
I had begun to turn transparent, translucent,
penetrable…Bless my soul!
I was sagacious. And that, not always.
Now they seem to ask me all sorts of questions:
"Tell us, what did you witness?
What did you see through? And why?"

So, I have already stopped wriggling
under the scourge of my free will.
There is nothing to admit.
Secrets fall off me themselves –
heart-shaped leaves, pierced by
Cupid's ray arrow. And I am
leaf-fallen, while above me,
through cold branches,
the bare vault of heaven
watches me like family…
I do not bemoan my lot,
nor do I triumph. I feel
in between this and that
view of life. After the bird
I await the stone. Then I'll
become a system fully open
under the jingling sound
of broken existence, non-
existence, just non…
And other glassy conditions.

THE STONE SHIP

A grassy hill –
pedestal for the clouds…
But Ale's stone ship
is anchored there.
All the Viking's Drakkars
have long been sunken,
rotting away or burnt down,
or wrecked against reality
like illusions. Only the stone
ship still plows through
voids in time and the ages.

The coastal imagery shines.
The wind is arguing with the ponds.
It calls them thieves of the skies.
—This is not a ship at all—
it flares up.—This is a megalith.
An observatory. Or maybe it's a
temple, or a tomb. But not a ship…

I raise the collar of my coat,
turn my back on the wind
because I want, somehow,
that desperate conqueror
Ale to have existed.
Even my heart is prompting me
that within me too there is a
sailing ship of stone
with a crew of secrets.

Even this grassy hill
encourages me through
some unexpected advents:
bulging like sails,
drowsy cows are grazing
on the northern lights.

HERMENEUTICS

Something confuses my thoughts.
Meanwhile, a fire is burning under them.
The way Mother used to boil homemade
soap during the war, a small biting fire,
over which an ashen sky with tallow clouds
is bubbling. Tears well in my eyes
from the smoke. I find it increasingly hard
to interpret what is dream, and what is real.

The bell rings. I run to the door.
There's nobody there. I pick up the phone,
and only a dial tone. No one from anywhere.
Yet they want me.

This turns into a small hole
as if from a 9 mm bullet –
something like a wound in the course
of the rest of the time –
something like the mouth of a whirlpool.
It seems that it wants to tell me something important,
but I'm already absorbed
by this native disorder,
and I don't hear anything else,
except the gushing forth of the future,
where someone is washing his bloodstained
hands with a cake of homemade soap.

EXHIBITION

Up the spiral staircase
of the Grand Palais
I suddenly got dizzy.

When I realized that after all
I was not going to fall down,
I told myself: Slow down, old man!
Apart from Hegel's spiral,
there are also other views of
elevation. So I began to pace
among the paintings populated
with cows, boats, and transitory faces.

I have seen this Constable
a hundred times, but only now
it comes to my mind that he
has meant to impress on us
how much more melodious,
clearer, and more noble
than us is nature.
Skies like mothers
bathe their baby clouds
in the tranquil water.
Is it a river or a lake?
Not everything in this world
is clear to me. But once the
horses drink from it,
it is not a swamp.
—Talk nonsense. Watch.
But don't touch the art!
the guard of the eternal halls
wants to say, but he can't wake up.
So, you can't distinguish him
from Constable's portraits.
But they are really "like living,"
like the present-day, newly rich,
fat-assed and thick-skinned,
thieves of aid for orphans,
thieves, who decry murders

After that, the paintings end.
It is raining outside. And I'm
surprised that there are no people
on horses and not a single guillotine.

IT SEEMS

*And it's a hard, and it's hard, it's a hard, it's a hard
and it's a hard rain's a-gonna fall.*
—Bob Dylan

It seems it is about to rain.
A lonely raindrop bursts in the dust.
"I haven't seen a bigger tear,"
the wind exclaims.
But why is it weeping?
Aren't we all wasted?

I seem to be sitting under the
shelter of an old bus stop.
But actually everything is buried
under a landslide of vapid time.
The last bus has gone.
And with it, the last teacher too.
What shall I do here? There are
no children anymore.
A secondary ignorance sets in.
The old plough has forgotten
how to plough. The old road
has forgotten where it goes.
Only the old earth remembers still.
But this doesn't seem to be on Earth.

They say, before he left,
the teacher was gloomy.
He bought a pack of cigarettes
from the little store, but only
to get change for the bus ticket.
He didn't buy bread.
Everything was clear.

Before he left, he looked for a long time
from the Mirabeau bridge, under which
silently flows Allami gulch.
Love also flows. And village women
dump their miserable garbage there.

"Master, where are you going?",
stonecutter Peter asked him.
"Calm down!", the teacher said.
Redeem your natural frontiers!
New ages are to come.

The bus will come,
and from it the new
teacher will descend...

The cloud comes down, and...
It seems it is about to rain.

CAPRICE No. 8

I repeat and repeat, as if
I am studying some lesson:
He, who forgets,
will be forgotten.
If you don't search the past,
you'll be searching the dustbins.
"Man ! That's magnificent !
That sounds... mighty."
Do you remember this cue
of a Russian tramp
who is searching
the theatrical dreams?
As soon as I wake up,
I begin to search thoughts:
a dream – a memory,
a dream – a memory.
I hang them like photos
on the wall of the staircase
between chaos and harmony.
Faces and women
returning from night shift.
There is no moon.
I'm looking for my mother's face.

TOWARD EVENING

1.

When the light leaves the sky
I think of you. Mystery closes
like a door studded with stars
and a lunar hoof fallen from the Centaur,
though at that time there were no hooves.
It is meant to bring happiness
now, when it's gone.

2.

Certain things leave reality
ahead of us. And we grieve for them.
Others will remain after we are gone.
I wonder, if there will be grief?

TRAIN

Exactly one hundred years after
his death Edouard Manet said to me:
"The train? Oh, it's train smoke!"

White and slow, and ruthless…

It doesn't leave, but disappears here,
it disappears within you. Though
you have vowed to remember it forever,
while after that…

The mature woman is looking at you.
She is not particularly broken-hearted
over your infidelity. While the child
has turned her back. She is looking
at the train. She doesn't know
that the train – oh, it's train smoke!

A FINAL TALK ABOUT EVERYTHING

Death is hiding in my home again.
I hear her pass along the corridor
at night. She goes into the kitchen
and drinks water from the glass jar.
Then I get up quickly, but I haven't
managed to catch any real trace of her.
The chandelier doesn't swing. The clock
is working and the world seems eternal.
Human speech flows like an open tap, and
this is Mom in the devastated children's room.
She is reading in a low voice, haltingly,
from some newspaper – not today's, and
just the titles. Just the large ones. She wants
to know if there's news and heavenly advance news.
Dawn approaches. The garbage truck is passing.
It lifts the barrels like an old alcoholic.
Then they open the kindergarten.
The Universe echoes with drowsy wail and cries.
Mom peers horrified from the window –
an underage future is shrieking and begging
the past to stay. Her old hand grips me.
"Where's Mom?" asks Mom.
"I don't like it here! And I don't feel like living!"
"Calm down," I say, as if to everything.
I smile because I hate maudlin scenes.
"It's time for breakfast now. There's tea,
and there are a few more teaspoons of sugar.
Think of something nice. Meanwhile, I'm
going out. I'll do something very important."
"No," says Mom. "Stay with me, and tell me first…"
"What?" She thinks long:
"Did your communism already set in
all over the world or does it still…"
I grow dumb before the talking relics.
I go out fast, the way one goes out
of kindergartens or of Eden's gardens.
Chiron pushes me away with his ore.
He summons her. I'm doomed
to living in the East.

FREE SKY

or the seventh death

Transparent and disorderly, and still warm,
the clouds are desolate. Did you sleep there?
Just a scent of sky and freedom from you remains.
And more, the silken ribbon of the sunset
has fallen from your hair.

Where are you? If you are looking for
your whisper, I took it away from you.
I'm holding it in the hollow of my hand
called soul. I'm holding it there like a cricket,
and he is singing quietly to me:

Love worth a song:
the dream of a child having kissed
for the first time the moon –
our teacher of lunacy.

Love worth two songs:
you and I, before we met.
Right?

Love worth three songs:
a clear ford, beyond which
there is no turning back
either in your parent's home
or in your old nature.

Love worth four songs:
the atavism of the heart.
A Thracian storm. A chariot.
An arrow aimed at heaven.

Love worth five songs:
the precipice of our self-oblivion,
and he, who falls, remains.

Love worth six songs:
from the ruptured lip
the taste of blood…

Love worth seven…

O, that's

the sacred,
the magic cat –
guardian of the Egyptian tombs
that has seven deaths.
And is watching us…
Hush!

Love worth a silence –
This is my love.
And you know it.

INFERNAL MACHINE

Don't fall in love with me.
I beg you, I order you!
Take everything you want
and run far away! Don't
fall in love. And leave!
For in a while the madness
will return to me and then
you'll hear other words,
another order, and another plea.

I'll tell you then what I'm
concealing now. Don't fall in love.
Don't pass through me!
I am a bridge, loaded with explosives
and the clock is ticking.
The unclear hour is overtaking me.
Every bridge between truth and beauty
is mined, doomed forever to be no man's.
You don't trust me? All right!
Just once more, press close
against me and you will hear
that time bomb.

Kiss me goodbye. Longer.
And run far away.

DEATH GALLOPING ON A PALE HORSE

*Notes on the white margins of
a catalog from an art show*

Turner had the knack of painting as he wished.
Yes, he's had the knack of painting like Rafaelo Santi –
far away serene horizons with promising serene skies.
Yes, he's had the knack of painting like the little Dutchmen –
land, water, and the sunny oddities.

Yes, he's had the knack of painting castles
amidst debris and delicious plants, like Watteaux.
And yet remain the very Joseph Turner…

You will say that everyone can paint
since someone has managed it before.
This is not as simple as it seems,
because Turner could paint like the
impressionists before they were even born.

Turner could paint like Matisse,
and like us. This, of course,
is not a great honor
but it's hard to explain.

As if not he but something else required
him to paint that way or otherwise.
As if we paint the light of history,
while he paints the history of light…
And that is why he doesn't care about our reasons.
I have no idea about his opinion politics.
He has painted the Battle at Waterloo
many times, but one can't say
if that is a victory or a defeat.

In the end, he painted his favorite
sea storms. He painted his favorite
mists, and suddenly – the skeleton
of death, galloping atop a pale horse!…

    * * *

The paintings that most resemble
the present day ones are the
frantic studies and sketches
for future painting.

There is something sketchy about
our time as well. We have been sketched
on the paper of transition.

Our fate looks more like the preparation
for a fate, like an attempt…
We are being erased.
They scrape us clean with the knife.
And they start us anew.
The artist fails to reach his ideal.
And it's a great deal to endure!
But we will endure because
our blood still holds the basic color
on time's palette. And our tears are
the sole link. But will perfection
triumph all the same? Will that dreamed-of
composition be completed?
And who will enjoy its harmony?
Who will be contemplating us?
When we are just a cloud of dust
behind death racing on a pale horse.

MIST

High on the ridge, mist.
I travel slowly, and I sink
into the wilderness where even
time stops moving.

Mist. As if I have encountered
a scoundrel vested in trust.

Mist, a broken pair of wings.

Even a blind man fears mist.

The yellow tunnel of the headlights
leads aimlessly. Whoever has passed but
has returned from the limits of death
describes his narrow escape this way.

Mist. I'm moving with great difficulty.
While fragments of reality float
along the roadside. A winter field,
Brown grass, the last pasture.
And hairy horses, pretending
to be grazing, or maybe they
are praying to our old,
age-old mother.

They kiss her wrinkled hand. And
foam drips from their bitter mugs,
and I stop looking at the road.
I'm looking at the horses.

Horses, an age old friendship.

Horses, faith and freedom.

Horses, useless, they say
to the world in which we live.
The world of isotopes and
the combustion engine.
The calculated world,
where horses are economically
unwarranted, or rather,
more clearly said, condemned.
You who are condemned, you
justices and forgotten ones,
pray that god will send you
a horse in the mist, a
friend in wretchedness.

I'm looking at the horses. I plan
to stop. To get out of the car.
I won't even close the door.
I don't want either to close or open.
I'll walk alone across the winter field,
past dark puddles, leftover snow.
I'll kneel down. I'll kiss the rocky hand.
But then, I hope the horses are real.
I hope they aren't made of dream,
of memory, or mist. I hope they aren't
an hallucination. I hope they smell of
stale sweat so I can mount one of them
and take my leave.

FOUCAULT'S PENDULUM

They ask me, both well-meaning
and not: how do I reconcile
the cold official obligations and
freedom? How do I combine the
clerk's stiff collar and the song?

I answer always smiling.
I answer: "The way all do…"

However, now, when I am
facing my own self, and
between me and me is only
this transparent sheet of paper,
this cruel screen of conscience,
I don't want and, cannot conceal,
this diarchy costs me very dearly.
Very dearly.
I envy trees, because
they don't have wings. Indeed,
they sort of wave their branches.
But this is just a game, not flying.
A dance of green. A prayer.
Confession to the wind god, this
fabricated, non-existent god.

For, if you see the trees flying,
pack up your things for the hereafter.

The trees remain forever faithful
To their nature. And it's the root. It's
the earth! And that inhuman permanence.

I likewise envy the birds, because
they don't have roots. Indeed,
their legs, outstretched in flight,
the claws, dug into nothingness,
resemble roots. But this is only
an illusion, a convenient pose—
such is our offensive view.
For birds remain profoundly
faithful to open space, to
eternal movement, and to impulse.
For their nature is the wing.

What shall we do, all of us,
who have both root and wing
deep within us (and beyond),
an omen of the catastrophic age.
And let me also say: an omen
for what is coming after.

From root to wing, this pendulum
provides a proof that the earth rotates.
White lava is flowing down my temples,
and I hear: somewhere in the caves
of my unfamiliar nature my
heart's explosions echo.
Hail, destructive elements.
Wings and roots, tear me
to pieces. All hail to you!

WITHOUT TEARS

For Stephan Danailov

How easy it is to be in love
at twenty. And how easy it is
to become the unbeloved…

I would embrace whirlwinds.
I would be kissing the rains.
I'd roll through meadows of
moist tenderness. And when
they'd push me down into
the fathomless "good-bye",
I'd think that I was dying.

But I'd be rescued by the
nets of youthful sun rays.
I'd jump on them the way
children jump on spring beds.
And my face would laugh
cooled by evaporating tears.
Girls like charms would coil
round me and I've felt freedom
best after the pain of parting.

But how awful it is to be in love
at forty and how awful
to become unbeloved.

Without "good-bye".
Without charms.
Without tears.
Parting doesn't
bring me freedom.

And I fancy I'm not dying.

AT HEMINGWAY'S HOUSE

Finca el Figia

Palm trees the color of cement.
Palm trees with black wigs
repeat themselves here
in a haunting refrain.
Palms-fountains
suddenly suspended
in the air…

Stop! Time has suddenly
stopped. This place is a
grave. The heart stops.
Muchachos, boys,
damn all false Santjagos.
Damn all barriers-rewards.
Introduce me to the sea.

And here I am, climbing up your tower, Ernest.
Somewhere nearby the bell tolls today.
America Central, America North and South.
Black poverty. Fury. Fury is essential.
But where is the vanguard, the lost generation?

You used to roam around like a celestial omen.
You used to hit like the Tunguska meteorite.
But an explosion followed, and the secret was
concealed. You were near, just a pace away
from our positions, but you sank into the drama,
into its blazing tongues. What were you?
A spaceship from another universe?
Or a falling celestial body,
a heart exploded with pain?

The once glorious yacht is now covered with
a tarp like a dead man after a street accident.

And behold, I'm climbing down your tower,
Ernest. And ever closer, the bell tolls today.

GALLERY I

ARTWORK BY

STOIMEN STOILOV

NEW WORKS FROM EUROPE COMBINE A MASTER'S TOUCH WITH AN ARRESTING VISION

The title of the mightily compelling Stoimen Stoilov exhibit at the Lyman Allyn Museum of Art in New London, "Window on the Black Sea – New Works," is perhaps confining. The collection of murals, etchings and lithographs might better be described as "The Carnival Ride We Call Stoilov's Brain" since, unlike many artists who paint only what they see or who deal in sheer abstractions, Stoilov filters both such sensory perceptions through the exotic baggage of his mind.

A contemporary Bulgarian painter and lithographer, Stoilov was born in Varna, Bulgaria, in 1944 and grew up on the coast of the Black Sea. He graduated from that country's Academy of Fine Arts and is now a resident of Vienna, Austria. His works are exhibited in many public and private collections throughout the world, and they display a paradoxically futuristic interpretation of the mysticism and mythology appropriate to both eastern and western Europe.

Fasten your seatbelt, then, and join the ghosts of other travelers who've apparently been inside his brain a while: Hieronymous Bosch, Albrecht Dürer, Pan and his eclectic and recurring entourage of Greco-Roman deities and myth-makers, Leonardo DaVinci and maybe the painter/patricide Richard Dadd.

Book-ended at either end of the Lyman Allyn's McKee and Chapel Galleries are two of Stoilov's massive murals. Along with a third, displayed at the top of the stairs leading to the exhibit proper, these murals serve as stylistic sentinels for the show. Actual rollable canvases, the murals appear, through the artist's skill and technique, as though they're actually frescos painted on some decaying wall certainly not found in the likes of Mystic or Darien. "Aged" through faux graffiti, cracks and coffee-like stains, the canvases are also fully realized and compellingly colored studies of various recurring motifs and allegories that pepper the smaller works comprising the rest of the collection.

The show is rife with images of various gods and a jester-hatted Everyman, horses and unicorn-like creatures, large Boschean birds, fish, fruit, flying machines, conical shapes, seashells and enough masks to supply the whole county for Halloween.

Said likenesses range in technique from the cartoony (as in "Horseman," pastel and gouache on paper-mounted canvas) to what seems like anatomy-textbook realism overlaid on graph paper ("Icaria" and "Mechanical Fish," both etchings with aquatint). Many of the lithographs are frequently depicted in triptych fashion – again a heavily and no doubt conscious reworking of the Bosch influence.

In companion pieces like the three lithographs in the "Mythology" series, there is a phantasmagoric discipline, as gleeful as it is ordered. The larger painting "Pandora" adds to the nervous freneticism with the suggestion of motion in stuttered images. On the other hand, clearly, some of the early, smaller works are at least in part studies for the murals that came later. It's interesting to see how the fragmented ideas actually blossom years later. It should also be mentioned that, in addition to his skill at rendering characters and objects, Stoilov's mastery of lithography—where, for example, with a simple, pale yellow wash and a few inspired slashes of red and gray, he suggests whole worlds of color that aren't really there—is extraordinary.

What does it all mean? Can you look at any of the pieces like a Rockwell painting and say, "Oh, gosh, is it already Groundhog Day again!?"

Hardly. It's easy enough to discern the tension and joy perpetually busy in Stoilov's muse. Sometimes they work together and sometimes not, but he's not afraid of the possibilities in either case. What the viewer takes from these rich and speculative histories is of course interpretive, but "Window on the Black Sea" is a nourishing exhibit.

Rick Koster
from "The Day", New London, CT

Green-Winged Horse

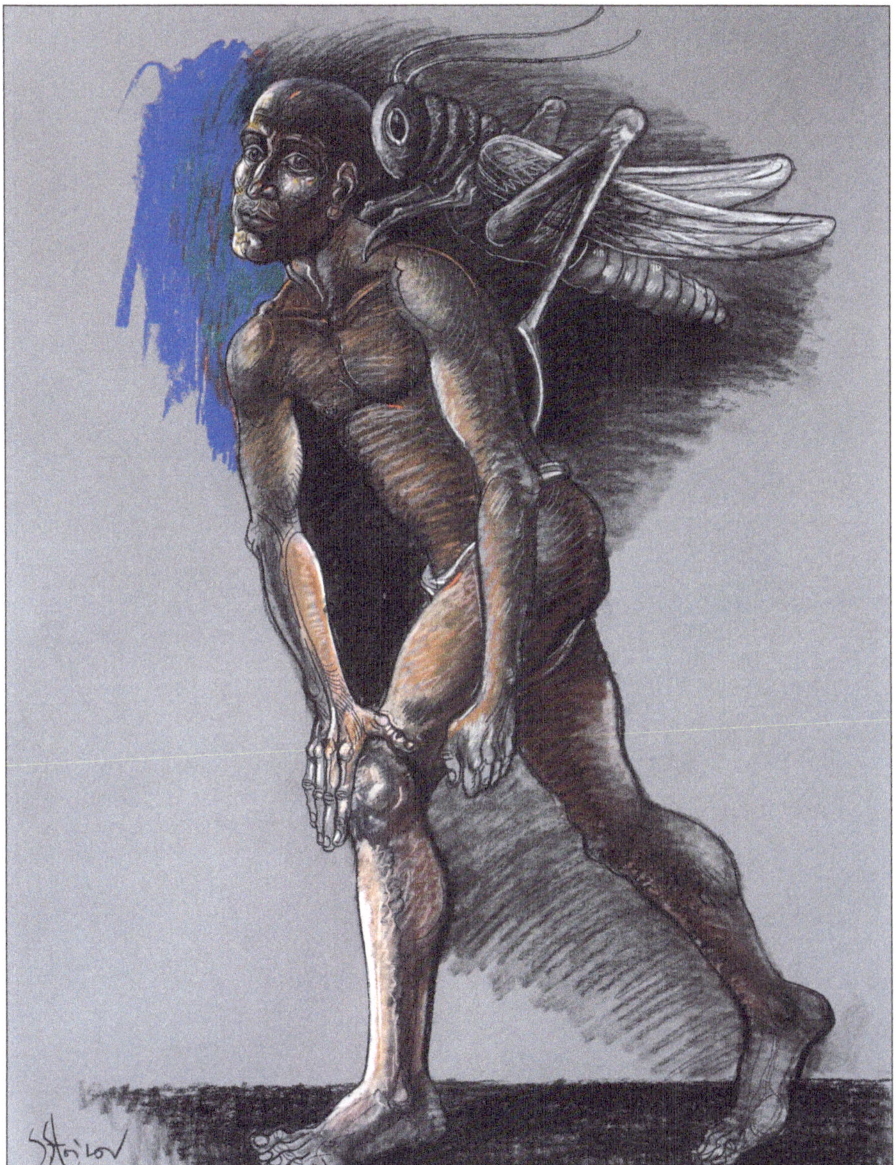

Green-Winged Horse

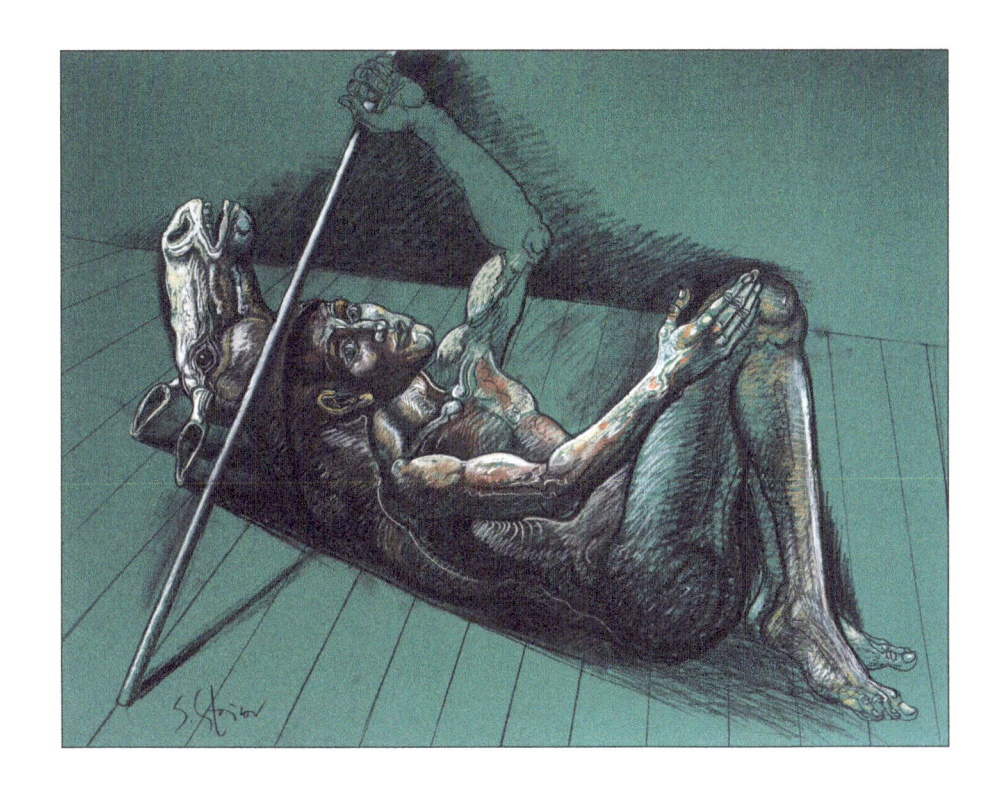

Gallery I

Green-Winged Horse

Gallery I

Green-Winged Horse

Gallery I

Green-Winged Horse

Gallery I

Green-Winged Horse

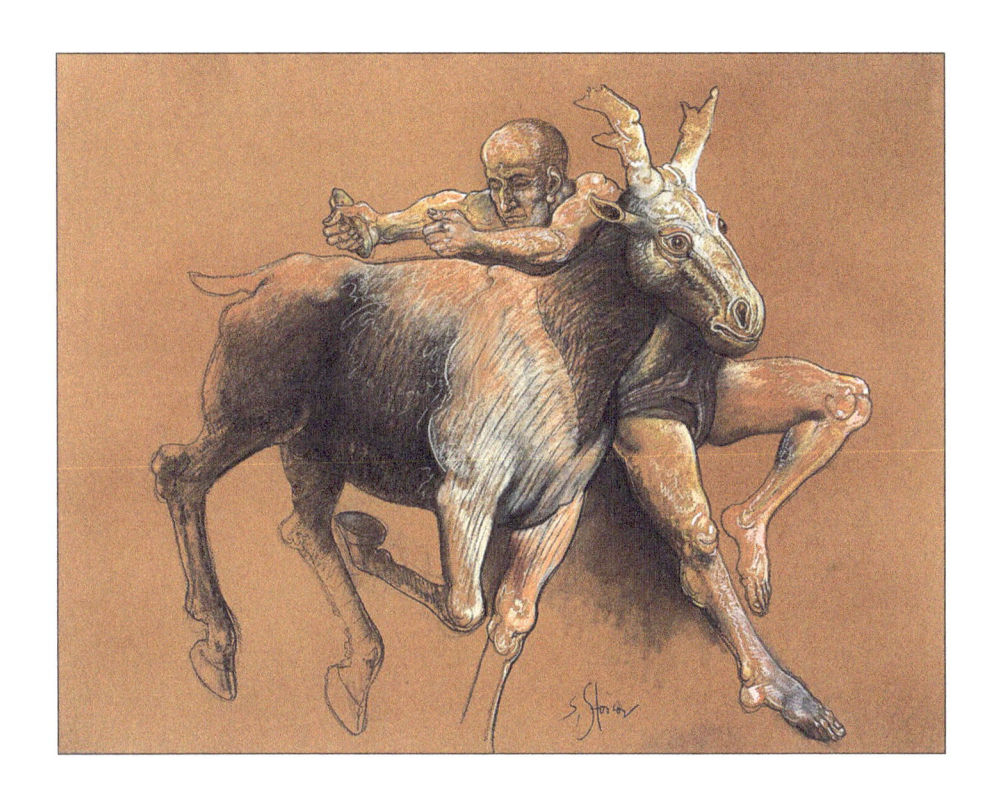

Gallery I

SKYBREAK

Selected Poems

FOREWORD

Recently William Meredith and I visited our old friend Lyubomir Levchev at his summer home in Serafimovo, Bulgaria, a village high in the Rhodopes range near the Greek border. As he piloted the little red Lada through the alpine mountains, he kept us entertained with stories of Orpheus, the namesake of his magazine and publishing house, who according to legend was born on one of the rocky cliffs. Though Orpheus' lyre became a constellation in the heavens, Apollo kept his dear remains on earth hidden on one of the mountain tops where the sun rises each morning. It was clear as Levchev spoke that he considered these stories to be only partially legend because of the spiritual realities they describe. And it was also clear how joyful he was to be back in his cherished mountains.

Skybreak is a kind of love letter to America, a brilliant rumination on the months he spent in New London while his wife was a fellow at the Griffis Art Center. It seems to have been a chance to put his life in perspective, to review the past and look to the future. In a remarkable six months he has given us wonderful new poems that detail his life there. Like Gulliver, he is able to see the landscape with the fresh eyes of the foreigner, explaining us to ourselves. At times, the poems attempt to capture humanity itself as it limps into the twenty-first century. Some of the poems are sad, others nostalgic, even despairing, but it is all right. Like Sisyphus, sometimes the poet must "roll a word uphill toward the summit of a futile song." These are earned poems, the insights of a very large soul working in a rhetorical or romantic tradition that an American reader may at first find difficult to comprehend.

In the Slavic heritage, a poet does not shy away from political statement in his song, nor is he afraid to speak directly to the reader of the things troubling his heart. Similar poets such as Lowell and Plath in our literature may have been eclipsed for the moment by the dictates of post-modern criticism, but the need for such song is as strong and eternal as the pull of the moon on the oceans. We are all lonely creatures sitting on this spinning ball. We need to speak to each other. The language of our best poets will always address this need.

Lyubomir Levchev's speech is informed by a metaphorical vision of great beauty and power, a poet's poet. The luminous sky at sunset becomes the "sky marshes." The Donne-like conceits of the love poem "Women Waiting for Ships" are striking. He speaks with exquisite ambiguity of the small turrets adorning the captains' houses where the ghosts of widows keep watch:

> Oh my beloved,
> awake from your sleep—
> I have returned.
> I enter willingly
> into the cage of fire.

The images are "crisp and sweet like this granite coast," as Levchev says in another poem. Their sweetness often derives from a surrealist sensibility.

> Bare maple trees fight each other
> with squirrels. A crumpled leaf, falling,
> skitters into church.
> Invisible ships, loaded
> with night, creak loud and sail away.

But the poet has a healthy sense of humor as well. Ruminating on his past as a high official in the government ("I used to meet the great ones, and see them off. / Now freedom and I are all alone together"), he decides that in the future he can always "earn a living washing flying saucers."

Lyubomir Levchev is one of the finest poets the Balkans has yet produced, attested to by his many awards. During the past six decades he has had over one hundred books published throughout the world. For ten years he chaired the Union of Bulgarian Writers. He is a member of the European Academy of Science, Art, and Literature, and was given the gold medal and the title "Knight of Poetry" by the French Academy. He has received the Pushkin Award, the Boris Polevoy Award, and the Award for Mystic Poetry "Fernando Rielo," among others. During his visit to Connecticut when these poems were written, he was made a Fellow of Morse College at Yale University.

Whatever his political or artistic future may hold, Levchev is clearly one of the great and lucky inheritances for the people of Bulgaria and now, through this volume, America. In a short poem entitled "Sun Ship," he observes a plane flying across the face of the moon like a bee that has fled from heaven and—resigned and earthbound—laments that "Someone else plays with the stars now…" It is not so.

—Richard Harteis and William Meredith
Uncasville, Connecticut

A STREET TO HEAVEN

New London Sonnet

A sudden street draws me unexpectedly.
I have never been here—yet I know it.
The familiar houses: I know who lives there.
I know that no one will ever dare
to walk to the end of that street
to see what is behind the pale
elusive edge of its perspective.
There are no houses, nor farmland beyond.
The last street lamp humbly bows its head
And peers, stunned, into the abyss.
The sky falls like a curtain.
Unreached. Resigned and unexpressed.
It could be a sign of the end.

My soul, you pretend to know something, again.

SKYBREAK

The real change of epochs is a change of
chasms. That granite shore
is the monument of a missing ship.
The specters of poets and the ghosts of sails
still appear, here in New England.
When autumn moons loom large
and the gold surge of maples
snaps our last anchors,
then Robert Frost is everywhere.
He was not from here
yet all here is from him.

In the forests—long stone walls.
Overgrown with moss, perhaps
they are the fences of forgotten
realms. Or maybe denizens
of a once-deserted chasm.
Our souls stumble. But Frost
passes through and destroys walls . . .
Between New York and Boston,
between Yale and Harvard,
being a poet is something
possible, insignificant and divine.
Emily Dickinson and Edna,
Robert Penn Warren, Lowell, and . . .
One might meet their ghosts
in a church, in a pub, or on some
invisible shore. Eugene O'Neill
sits upon a stone of the old
New London wharf and contemplates
the pale passengers of a missing ship.
We are all heading for the clouds.
Only Meredith descends from the sky
the way a Chinese manuscript unfolds
down a ladder of silk paper.
Every one of us has two worlds.
The first created us, the next will swallow us.
William has reigned over many a chasm.
And he presented this chasm to me:
New England—the secret garden of poets.
The dog named Mikey, a loyal Labrador,
leads me to the shore along a secret path.
Cardinals flutter in the branches.
And suddenly, shimmering in front of me,
is the hidden horizon.
Atop the three-mast ship are two words in Latin.
Unfurled by a gentle wind
they flutter. Two words: "Mare Liberum" . . .
Alive and well.

WINTHROP'S MILL

It is now only a reminder of its early days. Yet,
noting how poorly it plays the role of monument,
I would guess that its beginnings are sealed inside—
like a runaway slave escaped from a plantation,
or a shaman
of an Indian tribe—burned,
yet prophesying still. It is
not water but Time that turns the wheel.
The millstone of reason rolls
and grinds all to rubble beneath its weight.
A town is born.
Then set afire.
Reborn from the ashes,
it flourishes anew—and so on
and ever so. Everything seems crushed, fine ground—
Pequot, Nyantic, Nahmsok—
with a screech of worn-out metal.
Yet the memories of mills gush down the wooden leats . . .
Drawings of mills in an ancient book
show a knight tilting at windmills,
all unaware of that future time
when he would become me . . .
Fast-moving streams wind through meadows
where swallows, crickets, foxes,
still seek the rhythm of the mill.
It appears that all is ground down
except the world of the survivors—
that present-day labyrinth of metal overhead,
the bridge over the estuary,
and the Eugene O'Neill pier—where all is calm
and animals no longer fear man,
now only the wind has the right to tear off
branches. Hearths heaped high with grain
and answered prayers await their turn.

A band of reapers
spends the night beside the fire of an old faith
that tomorrow there may be bread for us all…
Our daily bread…
Crisp and sweet like this granite coast.

SO MANY RELIGIONS

To Betty Chu

So many religions. Such splendid temples.
Yet there is no solace for the mind . . .
The cold expanse
of the ocean
brings regards from Labrador.
Belfries—
golden steeples—
ampoules flung up to the sky;
needles,
piercing the world beyond . . .
The sunset may be a drug addict's dream,
and not a new beginning.

EARLY MORNING IN NEW LONDON

Clear skies prepare for sunrise,
birds and first light already a-quiver…
Thus creatures everywhere await
this hour of glorious promise.
Such is the shared faith
of peoples and plants,
spaces and visions. Now
the moon—Eastern dancer—
bows at curtain call.
Bare maple trees fight each other
with squirrels. A crumpled leaf, falling,
skitters into church.
Invisible ships, loaded
with night, creak loud and sail away.
Surrendering now,
swift gray-green shadows trail violet tails
to hover and hide
in the early settlers' graveyard.
These stone gardens were planted long ago
on the highest sites—below them
a glistening river. Above them…
(The sky is closer, that the soul may
more easily find its way.)
A gentle breeze heralds the arrival as I hear
the last whispering of ghosts:
"William is right, of course—
the eighteenth century is far better
than the twentieth."
And then the sun breaks
on the white captains' houses.

CLOUDS

To Charles Chu

Clouds, white and hunch-backed,
muffle the tolling of the bell.
As if to bear it away to silence
into the ocean's watery depths.

But the bronze oracle tolls on
for thee, for thee.
Holy oils anoint the doomed…
Alas, Heaven loved not John Donne.

The language of the universe
lacks words for "life" and "death."
A cold stream
becomes our way of life.

WOMEN WAITING FOR SHIPS

These white turrets,
perched on the roofs, were built
as waiting-posts for sailing ships.
They remind us of lanterns,
shattered cages,
from which the light has escaped.
They bring to mind the fragile
Greek phials that once held tears…

But such images today are empty of meaning
because we ceased, long ago,
to remember the sad purpose
of these small, solitary towers,
built for the watchful,
ever-waiting,
wives of sea captains.

Now other oceans captivate our minds.
Nuclear submarines vegetate
at their piers in Groton.
But they, too, are already
vain epitomes of time…

What is left, then,
to nurture us
as we ride the long waves,
and afterward?

All that is left is you—
Women—quiet, sad, and magnificent.
Women slender white towers.
Women, waiting for whalers.

You are our most enduring visions.
We may vanish.
You will never disappear.
Oh, my beloved,
awake from your sleep—
I have returned.
I enter willingly
into the cage of fire.

My cosmos is restored.
My heart sends a signal.
The lighthouse throbs with dactylic sparks—
Two short bright beams after a long spell of dark.

THE SUN SHIP

The sun ship fades away
majestically upriver.
I used to receive the great ones…
Now freedom and I are alone together.

After sunset the sky is still radiant,
but the streets are deserted.
I merge silently with the silhouette
of a world weary of insanity.

Someone else plays with the stars now
…Something else flutters above.
Like a bee that has fled from heaven
a plane flies across the face of the moon.

NIGHT TIME
or The Golden Saxophone

To the artist L. Posner

From the dark beyond, the night draws near.
The workday of the visible is over.
The woods turn into a cooling breath,
the brooks into currents of sound.
Outlines unravel and return
to the depths of the world...

America becomes its lights.
The single blinking neon signs—
America's nocturnal bees—change to clusters,
become golden swarms, embroideries, fantasies . . .
We seem to be flying through super-hives,
tasting honey distilled from lights.
It's not bad, not bad at all,
this neon liquid. Look!
Shining numbers—speeds, distances—
Shining letters—swooping by settlements—
write that light is courage,
freedom,
a thirst for stars...

The path toward new skies
imitates the shore's alien slope,
twisting like Louis Posner's gold saxophone.
He is unique, unstoppable—
Painting with sounds,
playing with colors.
I ask, does he understand the spluttering gutters?
Do they promise centuries of Spring?

He smiles: Any resemblance is coincidental.
Yet this inspires him with a Jazz theme.

And thus we unravel the remaining mystery.
Dora, Mary, Louis and, perhaps, I.
Perhaps ... a coyote runs in front of the car.
Perhaps ... in the comics of the night
I shall decipher
a secret sign from Destiny.
A melody clean as an otter,
The skeleton of a tractor in an asphalt barn,
the explosion of an ad along a long blank wall . . .

Dear Lord, how brightly we die in
Your unfathomable darkness!

PIANO BAR

To R. Harteis

Fantasia.
Blues. Fantasia.
In a piano bar,
      at an almost empty hour,
in a glassful of well-aged spirits
      the sparkle of diamonds…
How can the music be so pleasing,
while our century dies out in hatred?
There is no stage. There are no props.
      Inside that clean and tidy hall of glass
everything happens against the backdrop of a window.
The window overlooks the sunset—
sky marshes
      of blue light,
which you contemplate
      with innocent eyes.
The people sink within themselves,
      slowly, drowning.
History has not provided us
      with solid footing:
"You were not invited,"
      the gloomy quicksand murmurs.
We stand upon our hearts of stone
      not daring to step beyond.
Those who managed to weave themselves
      wings never did return…
Only the music helps us to soar,
      never frowns, never scolds.

The lid of the grand piano arches
      like the blade of a guillotine.
And you pass by. Casually, majestically.
      As only you can pass.

Da capo al fine—
Why not?
Why not—
Da capo al fine.

MOONLESS CALENDAR

The moon is an angel with a bright light sent
To surprise me once before I die
With the real aspect of things.
It holds the light steady and makes no comment.
—W. Meredith

    I.

Here come the days without nights.
Here come the nights without days.
The days that are deemed ...
Non-existent.
The nights about which ...
You had better not talk.
Instead,
you must hide them,
watch them secretly, from within your soul.
They never appear on memorial plaques.
They are like fugitives from some
non-human region,
natural cycles unknown ...
They are not listed on any calendar. With the exception,
perhaps, of one: the moonless calendar.

    II.

I name it,
Though I do not christen it.
So be it then.
May it find its own god.
But, the days ... Why can they
neither relent,
nor forgive?

    III.

Not a single non-migrating bird remains.
Not a single evergreen plant.
In the hail of acid rain, falling leaves
expose the fact:
there is no providence.

IV.

And when all collapsed, and sane men fled,
barrenness reigned in the land,
leaving me alone with a childhood dream,
and a band of lunatics.

V.

I had not seen them before.
I knew not who they were.
Yet. . . they would not leave me.
They kept returning.
And, in a glorious eclipse of meaning,
we entered the deluded forest together.

VI.

They were dark, mysterious, wretched.
Yet, unwittingly, they helped me.
In costumes and manners of other times,
they paced excitedly to and fro.
Passersby—handsome foxes—kept out of our way.
It seems that, of all extinct races, only one has survived:
the race of the passers-by.

VII.

Actually, I wanted to escape.
But where to?
Then I thought of the poet from remotest Lima:
Disgusted with laws and conventions,
(and not having partaken of *pisco*),
he begged
of his own free will
to be locked
in an asylum for dangerous lunatics,
that he might think, speak, and write as he wanted.

VIII.

My companions listened, disapproving.
No! They did not care for that poet's way of thinking.
They'd tried living in the "free will" of a mental asylum.

A romantic beginning,
until one realized that the head of the clinic—
sovereign of the ailing world—was essentially a madman

    IX.

It is discomfiting
to suddenly discover that fact
when he is grasping one's future
with one mad hand,
and, with the other, the key to secrets;
a key which locks in,
and never lets out.

    X.

Why do we fight?
A famous female philosopher
tried in vain to enlighten me at "La Coupole"—
Art is schizophrenia!
Power is paranoia!
One may not even shout:
O Lord, I am not worthy.

    XI.

That moonless page conceals the heart,
as once, in wartime,
women blanketed windows.
Viewed from outside, no one is there—
Yet, inside, one continues to live.
Within that dark and sheltered space
one's blind stars
may return, dazed but hand in hand.
For, if one rules—one takes the blows.

    XII.

Lightning strikes. The air is heavy with ozone.
Liberty herself
chose me to serve as tool.
The theater of eternity prepares for a new—
and quite unknown season.

MESSAGE

To Alia and Dima

Dimitri,
you have chosen fine stone
for the steps of the synagogue.
Not many people can uphold
their ideals till the end.

The New Year comes—
fifty-seven hundred and sixty-five years
since the conception,
the creation,
and the condemnation . . .
I am
older,
but my essence lies low.
The Mediterranean Sea
also claims to be sky-born.
Slave-palms are taming with green combs
the ruffled curls of the master-wind.
In cargo-holds old rats gnaw
at the sack of universal history.
And all the rational grains
are scattered.
"What we do know is but a tale
of constant shipwrecks
along the shores of that
which we do not know,"
say the salvaged rodents.
"We, the people, are more—they say—than…"
Clubs on the beach beam flames of music.
The ancient wharf is shining bright—
Antipolis awaits Hannibal…

Well, I must tell you, Dimitri, that I have no regrets
for wasted illusions.
I do not know if there is another kind of flying.

NEW LONDON RED

To Yvonne and Ken

The river flows into the ocean.
Above it, a quay of dreams—a crane of steel.
Stone temples.
Wooden castles.
Golden trees
heavy with the fruit of oblivion.

Everything in New London looks
out on the wharf, where an
emblem is enshrined—
with banners flying
the river flows into the ocean.

All of this is best seen
from the graveyard crowning the hill. Chased
by the late afternoon sun, the hill sails on
like the ship of a missing sea captain
Instead of a mast,
a centenarian maple tree
spreads its solitary shade.
As Dora sketched it, I wondered aloud
if we should call it the Tree of Life.
Pleased, the maple rewarded me
with a handful of red whispers:
"Who? . . . Where from?... Why?..."
I heard the blind force
crushing markers and gravestones,
grinding names to dust…

Lord Maple,
I come from the Antipodes.
Where they measure heads with bloody compasses.
And if one single head
stands out against uniformity,
it is hanged from the anti-maple.

"You know too much!
You think we are ignorant!
Soar up then! Go to heaven!
The Gods might welcome you as guest…"
They sent me up that way.

My new God is evidently shaken.
What else can he whisper to me?
He knows not.
He cannot say how I'll survive the coming day.
He only knows for sure
that heaven is not here.

Lord Maple,
it is enough for me
to observe the wharf
and arrive back into my self.
A neighbor of the clouds,
unidentified,
I will earn my living
washing flying saucers.

And, if this be Death,
the feeling is not unpleasant.
To be embraced by endless serenity,
to dissolve in a reflection of one's former self,
like a river flowing back to the sea

ANATOMY OF TIME

While we slept
the snow changed our universe.
Inside a room of many windows
we blink our eyes like bubbles in a cube of ice.
The oak tree that just yesterday celebrated
its golden wedding,
is now
a mythical white octopus
reaching out to snare us with its tentacles.
But, just in time, the house leaps back. "Look,"
she says, "that barely visible circle
under the snow,
like an incomplete equation,
is probably
the fountain.
What is that other shape, out there—
is that the scrapheap for unfinished tales?"
The red-hooded paths
have disappeared.
Perhaps because
the gnarling snow-ploughs,
prowling the grounds like wolves,
will soon go begging:
weather reports announce, from the sea,
a warming storm heading our way.
It will teach us a lesson
in the anatomy
of time.
The giant tree will blacken
like the fossil of a lightning strike.
Hunters will prey on animals.
And beneath the snow we'll find again
the baby doll, lost long ago…

Why do we love the snow?
We should rather fear it.
Why do these innocent white scenes
seem to take us back to heaven?
Perhaps because
our notions about all things
are only shapes under the snow
until the melting rain
lays bare our fantasies.

WINTER RAIN

When I let myself be sad,
it means that things are still in order.
The message may be scrambled, but I can tell.
The treacherous winter rain drizzles driz… zles… izzles…
and the world seems made of brittle glass, revealing
its crystal voids and icy peaks…
In the forest, King Arthur's lake is silent.
Beneath the icy mirror surface of the water
lie golden, bloody, brown, and even green
leaves—silenced mouths. As well as
stones—the indifference of friends.
A Byzantine mosaic, inlaid with
cannons and tracings of lovely women, and…

Why does the rainy winter weep?
The lake will speak. The leaves will leap
back onto the stubborn branches. Limes will scent the air.
And the shallow stones will be laid bare…
Yet will that thin ice… melt away?

SPRING IS BORN

To James Michael Tripp

"Spring is born in the air"
the birds tell me joyfully.

Elsewhere
it is still cold and bare.
The hilltop like a child's knee
swabbed with iodine.

I would like to be a winner again.
Winning a game of cards, at least,
at home
tonight,
playing against Fate with a tired pair of hands.
While the wood in the fireplace crackles
because it's wet—wood gathered after a storm.

I yearn to be a winner again,
to have the joy of telling those birds:
"History is made by winners,
art—by the defeated!"
And afterward I will squander
whatever I have won.
Squander it…
Even sell my labor
in a factory for Spring.

FLYING AWAY

I think about flying away. I see
the sunset as the autumn of the skies.
Frost-tipped red light sweetens the air one last time.
A sigh becomes a prayer abroad.
I roll a word uphill toward the summit
of a futile song.
God surely speaks a different language.
And I do not know how much I understand.
It seems He has not created us,
but has merely admitted us
into His lonely meditations…
And now He has regrets.
But it is late.
Too late now.
The sunset is quenched. Longing is never quenched.
Clouds sink. Submarines leave Groton.
And night-flakes are falling like black snow.

A POET IN NEW YORK
at sixty

> *Asesinado por el cielo,*
> *entre las formas que van hasta la sierpe*
> *y las formas que buscan el cristal,*
> *dejare crecer mis cabellos.*
> —F. Garcia Lorca

I am attracted by the repudiated city.
It emerges from the sea in the morning. At night
it hides in the sky. Golden,
a huge window without curtains,
no staircase leading to it.
No apprehension
that someone, in the darkness, is watching.
God is busy. "God gives
money," claims an unforbidden sect.
Not to the poets, though. In the shade
of a pyramid
or a skyscraper
those scribblers register dreams.
They record the hopes
of self-invented pharaohs.
The air is sweet with magic.
Brodsky, brooding, roams the streets
and Ginsberg pokes at shavings scraped from the sky.
New York is filled with poets prodding the absurd.
Loving the city because, in its monstrous size,
it lets them be…
One more…
Or one less…
It loses significance
with the melting of the blood-stained snow,
when the grass sends up once more
its green subpoenas.
We breakfast on the lawn
on the bread of our illusions.
Summer skaters are already racing
in the lanes of Central Park.
My April creeps closer, like a cat
stalking a mocking bird.
Hey, fly away!

PORTRAIT OF A CITY
mantled by a storm

To Frances S. Tripp

Is that a city or a relic of a different era
washed up on the today's shore? I still can't tell.
Its old name, Nameok, meant fishing ground.
But the whales swam off and nuclear subs were spawned.
The main street starts at the wharf
and proudly bears the label "Captain's Walk".
The vacant antique shop
is called the "Captain's Treasure".
"All that is doomed belonged to captains,"
squawks the talking parrot.
Both sides of the street are crowned
by sparsely visited cathedrals—
granite-gray across from brick-red.
They are the highest buildings,
rivaled only by the Mohican,
a once-posh hotel. Within its premises
the arts of defeated tribes are exposed for sale.
As you enter, something gently strokes
your forehead, long a stranger to caress… You shiver.
Eagle feathers dangle from a thin hoop.
A magic web is trapped inside—a net
woven from the lines of Indian fishing rods.
"Is that a shaman's pendant?" you will ask.
And they will explain that it is
a dream-catcher. Handmade.
Price—thirty-nine fifty.
When you turn to leave a storm blows up.
And you realize that you are the dream,
and they have caught you in the trap.

In New London they say "If you don't like the weather
wait five minutes and it will change."
But you are a dream… Arid, in dreams,
time only flows, obeys no laws.

Fiery harpoons strike in the captain's sky.
Clouds are the ghosts of whales. Their thrashing
tails snap the tall masts of whaling ships.
When the sea sweeps you off the blood-stained deck,
you sink in a tide of darkness .
Then will you say, "Dear, did you notice

the darkness passing through our souls?"
What a frost of solemn lies!
"My life shuddered
like an aircraft penetrating a thundercloud,"
you will say later... By now you are
cast ashore. Flotsam from a different era.

A city, built with tenderness on a land of destroyers.
A deserted dream . . .
People disappear here, at the end of the day,
As if they, too, had sunsets.
The poetic dusk lingers.
A portrait, forever unfinished.

Mother of dreams,
I beg you, don't wake me!

RUTH

The sapphire—of fiery, blue, or golden hue—
is the gemstone of creativity.

Sapphire House is situated
in New London, at 33 Granite Street.

For long years it was called
The Armstrong House.
Who was he?
A merchant
of boat sails, perhaps?
They no longer remember.
But the clouds are knit of his fibers.

The house is majestic, three-story.
Here wood plays the role of marble.
The ionic columns make the entrance

seem piously reverent.
But the rear walls more closely resemble
the shaggy coat of a forest magician.

People enter and exit,
play their parts and disappear.
There is only one permanent resident:
the ghost of the house,
named Ruth.

She throws cutlery.
Shifts furniture.
Gulps French wine. And makes
indecent appearances to sleeping boys.

People seem to dislike Ruth.
They fear her. They ask themselves—
How many centuries has that child lived?
What does she want…

I will stay here for a time
and then I, too, will disappear.
A pale globe shines in the sky. I can see
a halo—the radiance
that used to predict a change in the weather.
And in that lunar
globe
floats the heart of a dead god, preserved in spirits…

Ruth,
we know each other well.
You are that ironic force,
which forever rearranges
the things inside us,
and us inside the things.

Ruth,
Shift our furnishings again!
Shuffle these words for me!
Shuffle the images of the world
and deal them once again!
Perhaps this time I will be dealt
the wish-card I have so long sought,
with that sightless child in mind…
I delve into the sapphire night.
Stars rain. And I am close to God.

AT THE HIDEAWAY INN

To Niles and Pamela

Teach me once more, God,
the poetry of silence.
    —Niles Bond

At the end of the world,
the end of illusions,
the end of my life,
I have found my Double.
And he thinks he has found me.
In front of us, two icy glasses of tranquility.
Inside us, misgivings that we may not be so alike.

Here the Lieutenant River overflows its banks.
And I can see him, slim and ironical,
against a background of swaying, gold-brown—
I am told it is called Elephant grass.

We wade cautiously
into the stories of our lives.
There are shared experiences, but
our destinies were not the same.

Why, then, are we Doubles? What likeness did we
discover in ourselves with such surprise?
Like visions? Like passions? Like hopes?
He tells me about his incurable youth—

He loved music, graduated diplomacy
(composing notes of a different style).
He never got used to the applause of cannons,
and was only aware of the refuge in poetry!

For him, the war ended somewhere in Italy…
"Is that so?! Did you meet Ezra Pound?"
"No," he says. "He was a master wordsmith,
but he discarded poetic taboos too soon…"

And thus, on creaky floors of Japanese castles,
through lush Brazilian jungles, we walk together.
Beneath our feet, a rainbow burst of flames;
around us, enamored sounds rising like smoke.

Poets today suffer from immune deficiencies.
Clarity kills them like cyanide.
God, abandoning empty words, retreats
with my Double in the silence of the Tablets.

"Wait," I cry. "Perhaps I have discovered
what makes this magic. Perhaps both of us
are sound and color, occurring together,
coinciding in the overall range of sound/color."

I have always believed in these miracles.
Have always believed that, suddenly and with dignity,
different people, under different skies, will
recognize at the very last that they are Doubles.

THANK YOU AND GOODBYE

To Dianne and Dennis Slopak

Dennis invited us to stroll the paths of his childhood.
It might be a picnic. Or it could be a trial,
in which the jury passes judgment.
Is there deceit? Everything seems to be the same—
and yet to have changed…
There—the waterfall—the Devil's Hopyard!
Once a wild adventure, now
tamed with rails and labels.
The water's sound recalls the babbling of a guide
repeating boring tales of Mother Nature's genius.
The cascades tremble
in yellow hues like the fingers
of a chain smoker. We reach for a box of matches—
in this park East of Eden,
all evidence of our presence,
all clues to our outdoor feast, must be erased.
We burn greasy paper bags and paper napkins,
stained with what looks like blood but is only lipstick,
and the leftovers. Remains. Remains! Not easy to burn.
As their name, in fact, suggests:
we are leaving, they will remain . . .
An old covered bridge links the banks
of the famous Salmon River.
(The scent of rotting wood reminds me of Grandpa's cottage.)
There may be golden fishes here
but fishermen have all this glory for bait.
There is no other path! Our era is fated.
We keep strolling in the forest
that claims to have inspired the verses of Frost.
Autumn turn out to be the Queen of New England.

Yet Spring is the fairy godmother.
And Dennis leads us skyward along a reckless slope.
Long ago, railway lines ran through here—and trains,
laden with angels, puffed away in a heavenly trance.
What remains of them today
is only a few steamy patches of loco clouds
and this reckless slope.
We climb down the ravine to the dry riverbed.
Everything—from the soles of shoes to the secret soul—is filled
with detritus. Twilight and parable of a poisoned stream.
The walls of this gutter are scrawled all over with porno dreams—

reminders of a hippie colony, whose world
has also been dismantled . . .
Dennis' childhood
seems to be running out. The jury is inclined
to recognize the changes lege artis.
The fairy-tale path ends abruptly on the shore of an allegory.
And the ferry drifts toward us as in the verse of Alighieri.

MAP OF THE WORLD

To Tzvetan Marangozov

In a waiting room—
crowded with the sense of being alone
within the temple
of inner and outer space.
A crumpled newspaper
lies like a fallen angel.
The draft of entrances and exits
reminds me
of fleeting fate.
All vehicles pass through such
crossroads. Even God
descends in his machine.
And Eternity ends in a miracle.
You have the feeling that something is missing,
Something essential has left. . .
You still believe, yet
you no longer see the familiar perspective.
The view has changed, migrated perhaps.
How elegant and full of sun

was our perception of the Renaissance!
Uccello. Fra Angelico. Mantegna . . .
And, at the far end—de Chirico.
(I knew him.)

Here there is no perspective.
Instead
they have crucified a map of the world.
A map like a played-out card.

You can feel the wrench,
as if cutting and stretching a child's ball...
You do not care for map-reading,
yet you stare . . .
And review the old lesson:
how the land cracked and how
the continents drifted apart. . .
The coastline betrays their kinship.
It resembles a banknote torn in two—
that the halves may someday
identify their bearers.

Yes. There is a sudden urge to run away.
Yet you stay.
And, seeing the familiar oceans
from the other side,
from a room filled with
unknown waiters, unknown place-names,
you understand that urge to run.
You find sanctuary
rooted in your own peninsula,
    in your Balkan-ness,
    in your "Ego."

What are you waiting for, friend?
The other coast?
Or the second half of the bank note?
Who are you waiting for while you bleed
at the perception of break-up, separation, dispersal,
of dreams torn asunder...
That wrenching disruption of the universe . . .

The years come to the farewell party—uninvited.
Yesterday's memories weep aloud.
There was a time... We were running away from stern fatherlands
Today those fatherlands, friend, are running away from us.

THE DESTRUCTION OF GOMORRAH

Everyone talks about Sodom.
Nobody mentions Gomorrah.
Why?
Because it got second billing.
Salt pillars
curse your home.

Before History opened
its toothless mouth,
the fear of truth had done its job.
Instead of the Past, the passer-by—
ever the gloomy witness—casually lets you know
that near Vladaya they eliminate words,
kill rhymes,
destroy books.
Between two quiet mountains
an evil highway has arisen.
Dangerous clouds haunt the air.
Storehouses?
What is their purpose? No one knows.
Yet they are stuffed with books—
doomed to be recycled.
The work is quick, follows a secret schedule.

The soldiers selected for the job
must be brutish, illiterate,
that they may not know who is dying.
They will tear off the hard covers
like innocent children ripping wings
off butterflies, or birds.
They will load the mutilated bodies
of books into sealed freight-cars.
Books by Plato, Lenin, Slavcho Transki,
Shakespeare, Rastsvetnikov, etc., from which
some factory will produce
toilet paper.
The elements are cruelly indiscriminate.

On the battlefield of the routed epoch
I walk among the corpses of books
like a father seeking his children.
I cannot find them.

I am stained with the blood of ideals.
Suddenly I become the father of all

the doomed, denied, convicted
words, which will be mixed
in the stomach of the factory for oblivion—
Lies and justice, Glory and infamy…
Earned relief for accursed Gomorrah!

I may not object to that theft of time,
nor the grass that grows because of me.
But I cannot envy those whose behinds
will know so much more than their heads.

GALLERY II

ARTWORK BY

STOIMEN STOILOV

WINDOW INTO TIME:

The art of Stoimen Stoilov

Aside from his paintings, the best way to get to know Stoimen Stoilov may be to have lunch with him some aquamarine afternoon along the Black Sea Coast in Varna, the town of his birth. There, over fish and white wine, he will tell you stories of this ancient sea coast like some modern day Carl Jung or cultural historian. But Stoimen's vision is that of the poet, not the scientist. The freighter drifting by on the horizon with the barely discernable and oddly-shaped boxes on deck is carrying sheep to Perth, he will explain. Sheep, of all things. It could as easily be a Phoenician cargo ship or Argonauts sailing on their way to war. He knows all the many civilizations that have made their home in this region. Orpheus was born in the Rhodope mountains, he explains, and even now archeologists are searching for the lost city of Atlantis in the depths of the Black Sea. As in India, these lands have been inhabited for so many centuries the air is thick as a winter fog with human spirits.

In the Balkan tradition of mystics such as Vanga, or the earlier oracle found at Delphi, Stoimen Stoilov seems able to tap this collective unconscious, moving in and out of time, backward and forward like the great white fish that swims through his paintings these days, carrying all of civilization on her back. One recalls the great turtle of Pacific Ocean legend which shoulders the whole universe, or even Melville's great white whale - similar archetypes for the mystery of our tenuous human condition. The passengers astride Stoimen's great fish, a rowdy band of Mardi Gras revelers, toss off a cornucopia of human artifacts, soiling her wake as she makes her way through the oceans of the cosmos. And if these oceans seems vast and empty, there is the consolation that we are all traveling together, have each other at least, for better or worse, as company on the journey -- it was his making as an artist, Stoimen will tell you, when his professors dismissed him from engineering school for drawing caricatures in class, letting him spend a year's sabbatical on the beach listening to the song of that beguiling creature.

Watching Stoimen's eyes scan the waves that afternoon, I thought of William's poem recounting the two masks unearthed in Varna, the poet's awe for those ancient masks whose curious eyes are fashioned from the oldest known gold ever to be worked by prehistoric artisans.

> When God was learning to draw the human face
> I think he may have made a few like these
> that now look up at us through museum glass
> a few miles north of where they slept
> for six thousand years, a necropolis near Varna.

What was Stoimen watching, what did the artist intuit as his gaze drifted out to sea?

> It is moving, that the eyes are still questioning
> and no sadder than they are, time being what it is—
> as though they saw nothing tragic in the faces
> looking down through glass into theirs.

This same humanity, the same outward longing is transparent in Stoilov's work through the clear window of his imagination. But his is not a facile optimism despite the sympathy one finds there for his fellow human beings. Like William Meredith, Stoimen does not shy away from the dark underbelly of life. For two years Meredith lay unable to move or speak after his stroke. At the height of his career Stoilov's studio was mysteriously burned to the ground along with his life's work. Each man has had his share of trouble you might say. How does one transcend such history, achieve the sort of grace with which each man now lives his life?

The early work, in particular seems to tell a more ominous tale. Were those rigid characters with fractured faces and stately miters in etchings he did before 1989 actually symbols of tyranny, I asked him, thinking how poets were forced to speak in metaphor during the Stalinist period of Bulgaria's history?" Art responds to politics, of course, he agreed, but his concerns seem to run deeper than the vagaries of political life.

> Only clay and gold, the ancient masks seem to say
> passing through one condition on its way to the next.

And what of the strange animals that seem to pervade so much of his earlier etchings? Like Picasso and other contemporary masters, Stoilov's work sometimes takes its inspiration from more primitive cultures - he has, in fact, lived among aborigines in Australia - where the experience of the tribe seems at once most simple and most profound, where the human river seems to run its deepest. The paintings come magically alive like the beasts on the walls of the caves of Lascaux in the firelight. We may have no idea of what language our primitive ancestors may have spoken, though the images they created to "name" the beasts, or bring them down, tame or even worship them haunt us still. In Stoimen's work we are entranced by the creature's bright eyes, so tender and strange, that seem to look on with such wonder and pity for the evil man does to man in the name of authority.

Far from naive, these works reflect a richness and a mystery that flows out like the rings on the surface of a lake when a heavy stone is dropped into the center, or if you wish, Pandora's box, spilled out onto our laps, helter skelter, come what may. Though bruised by what they see, the eyes are filled with compassion finally, that remarkable charity that informs all truly great art.

After lunch the day we visited Stoimen—fact always stranger than fiction, as though it were ordained—I chanced to meet a woman swimming in the ocean named Stoimenova. As we swam, she explained that the name Stoimen in Bulgarian meant something like "stay name" in a household where too many children had died young, an injunction that the child live on and his reputation not die. I thought how aptly named our painter friend is, for certainly Stoimen Stoilov will not be forgotten any more than other native sons of Bulgaria who have become citizens of the world and masters of their art.

Richard Harteis
Fulbright Poet-in Residence
American University in Bulgaria, 1995-96

Green-Winged Horse

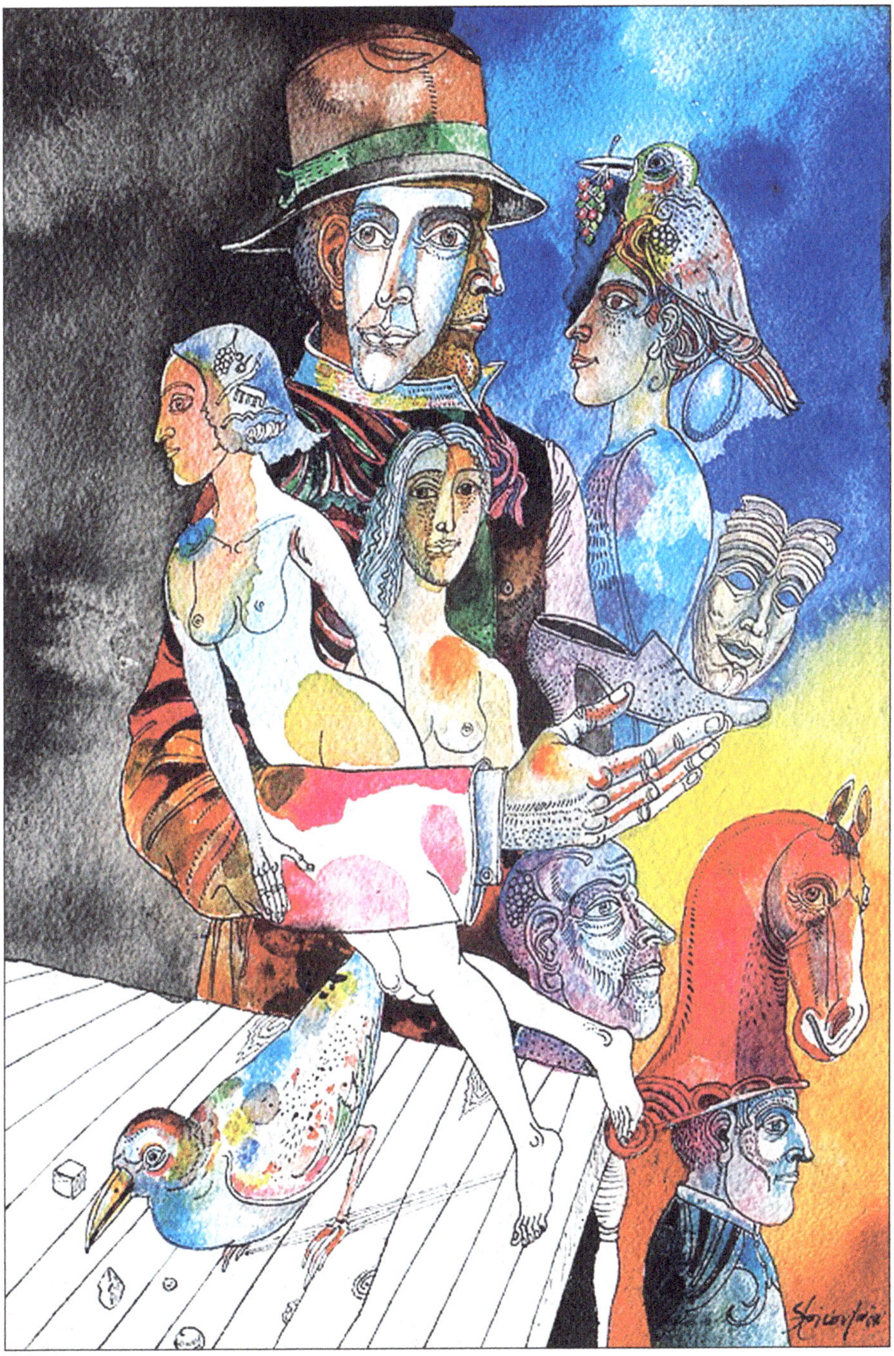

Green-Winged Horse

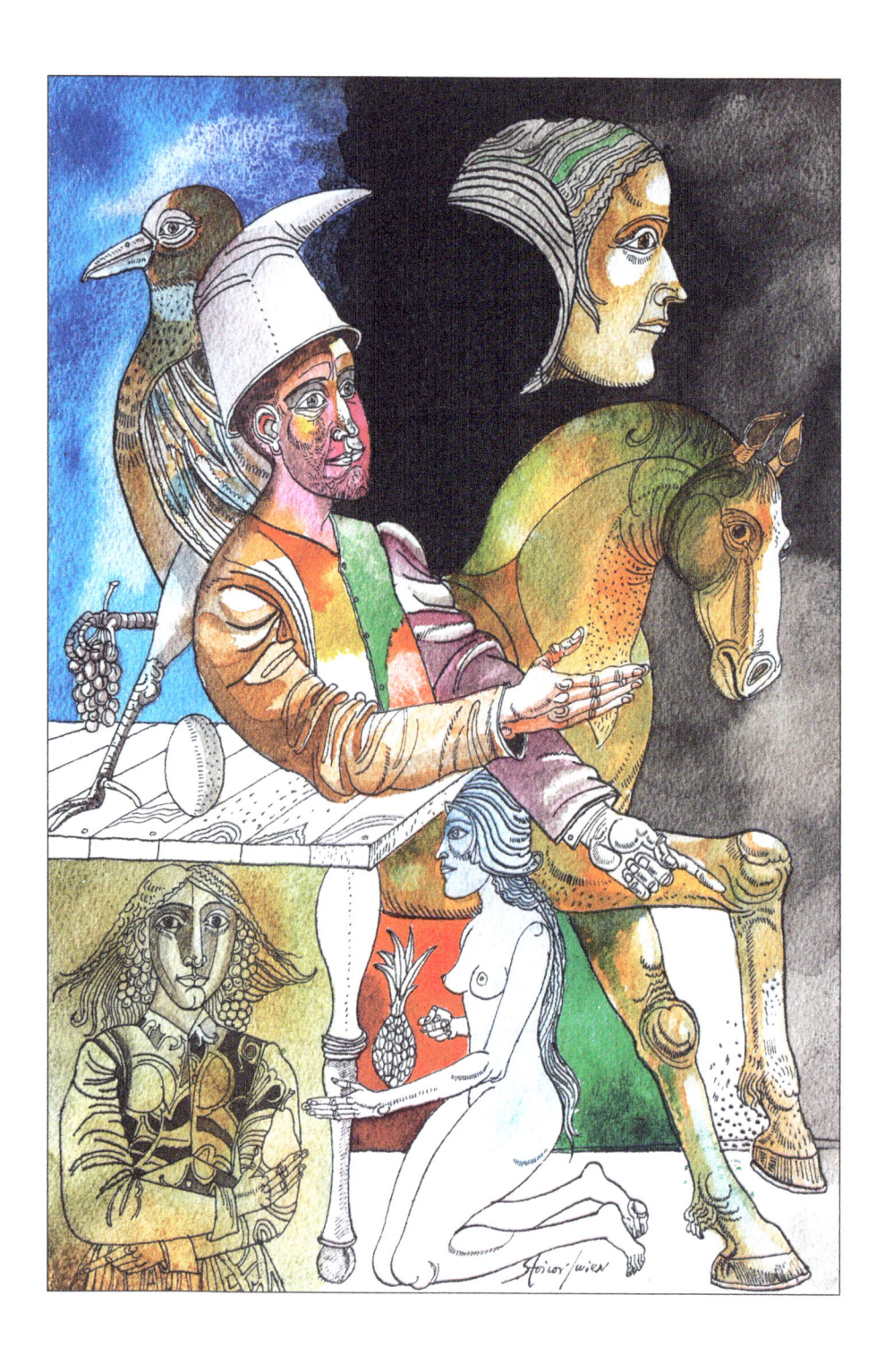

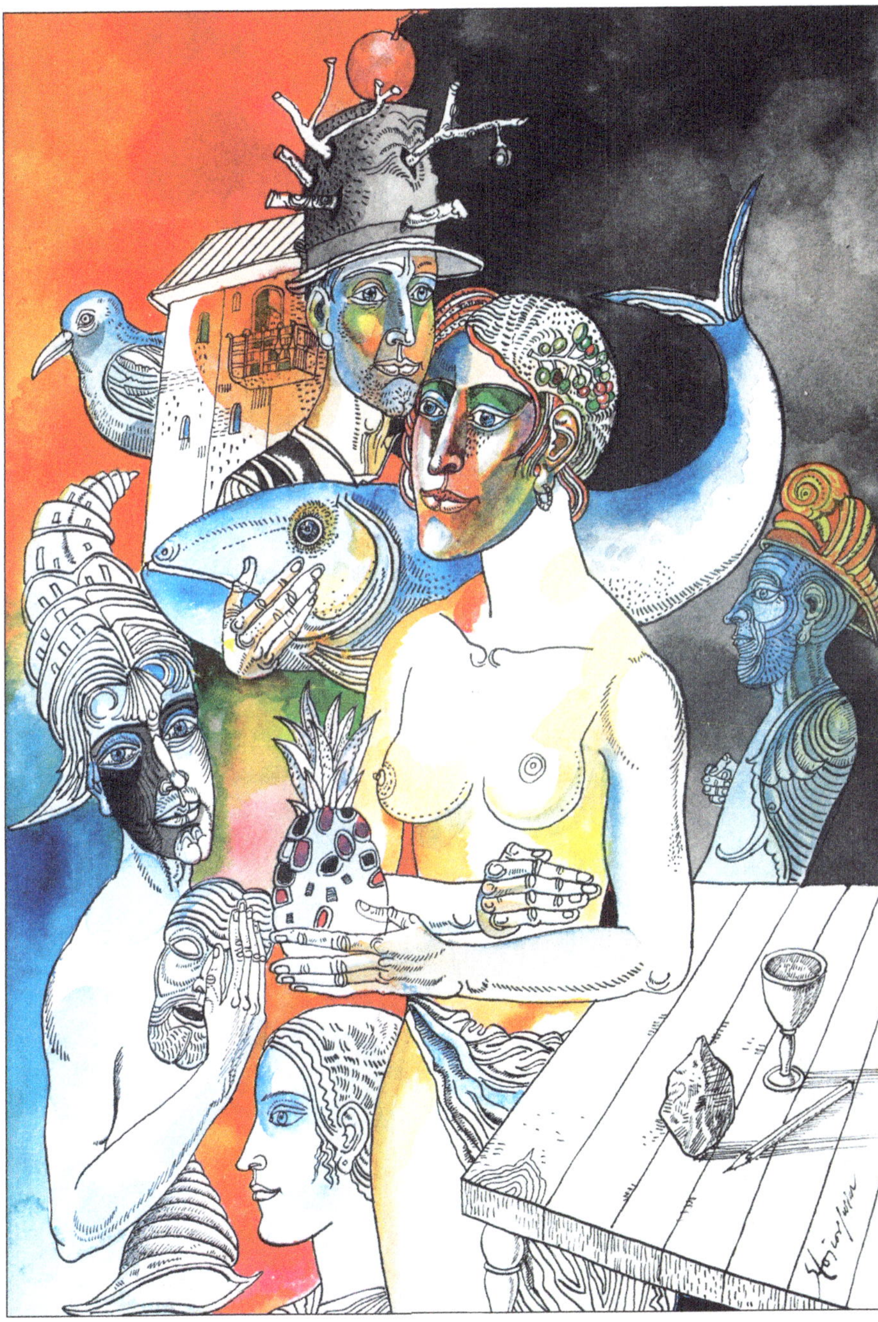

Green-Winged Horse

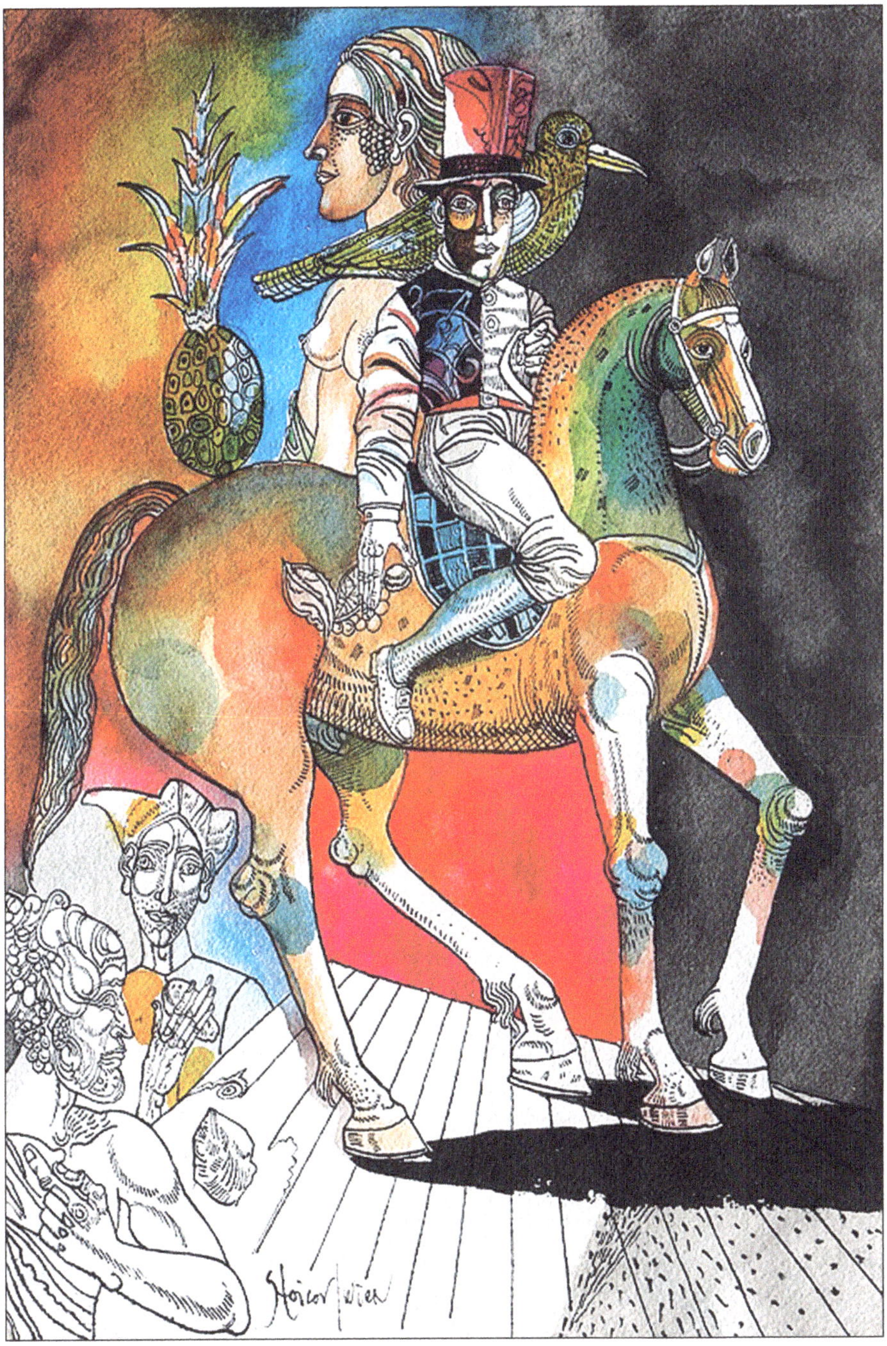

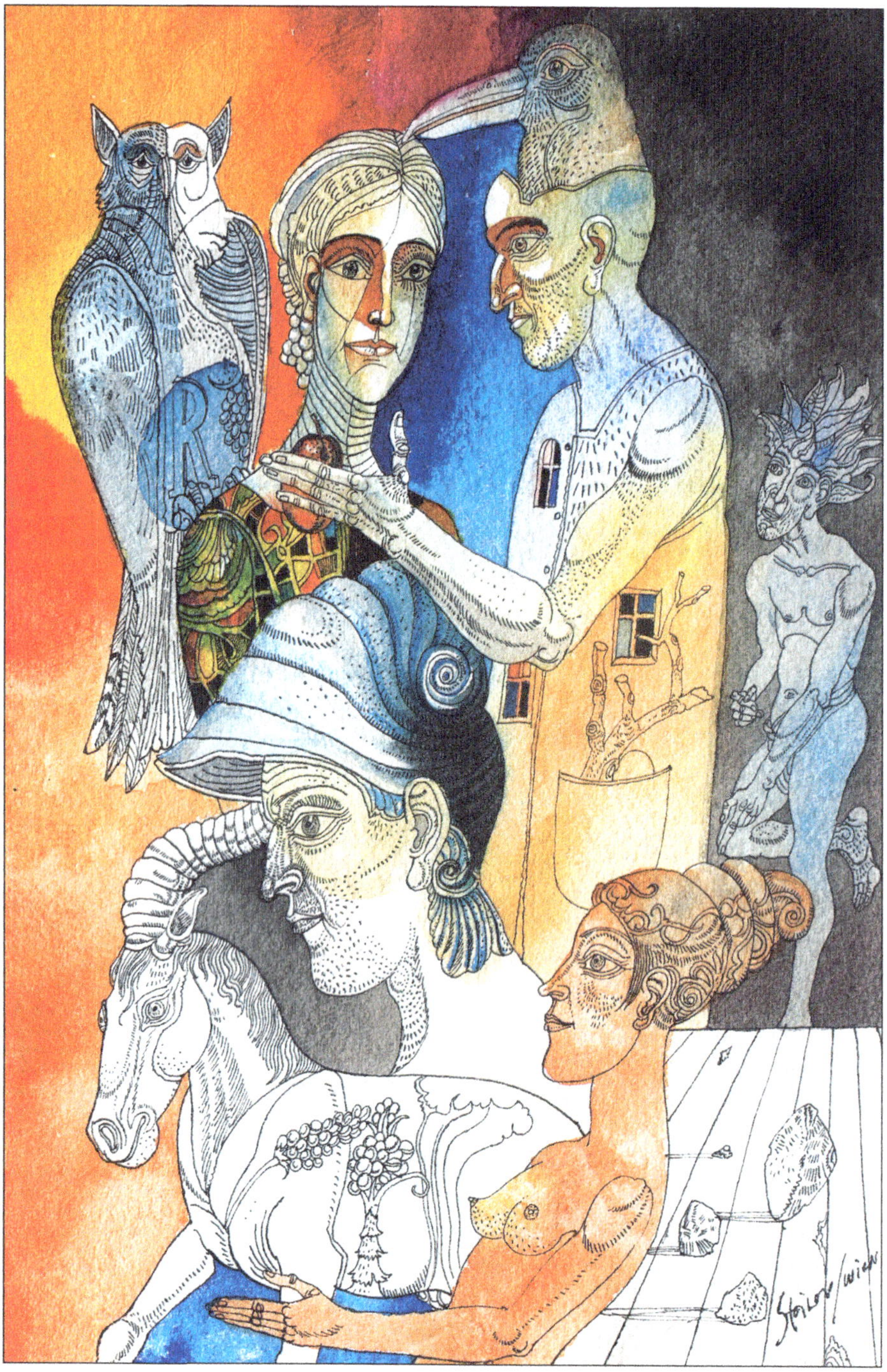

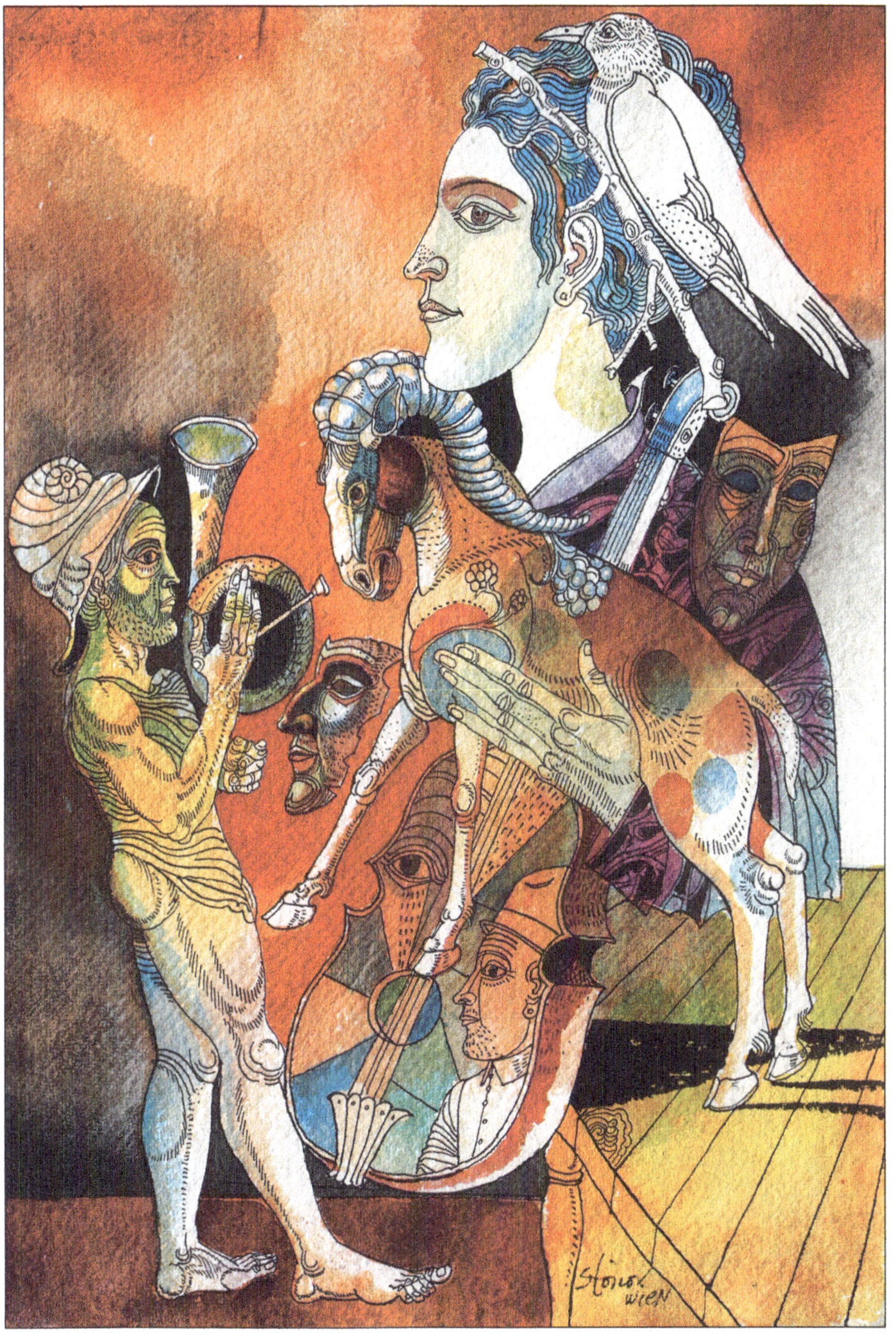

Green-Winged Horse

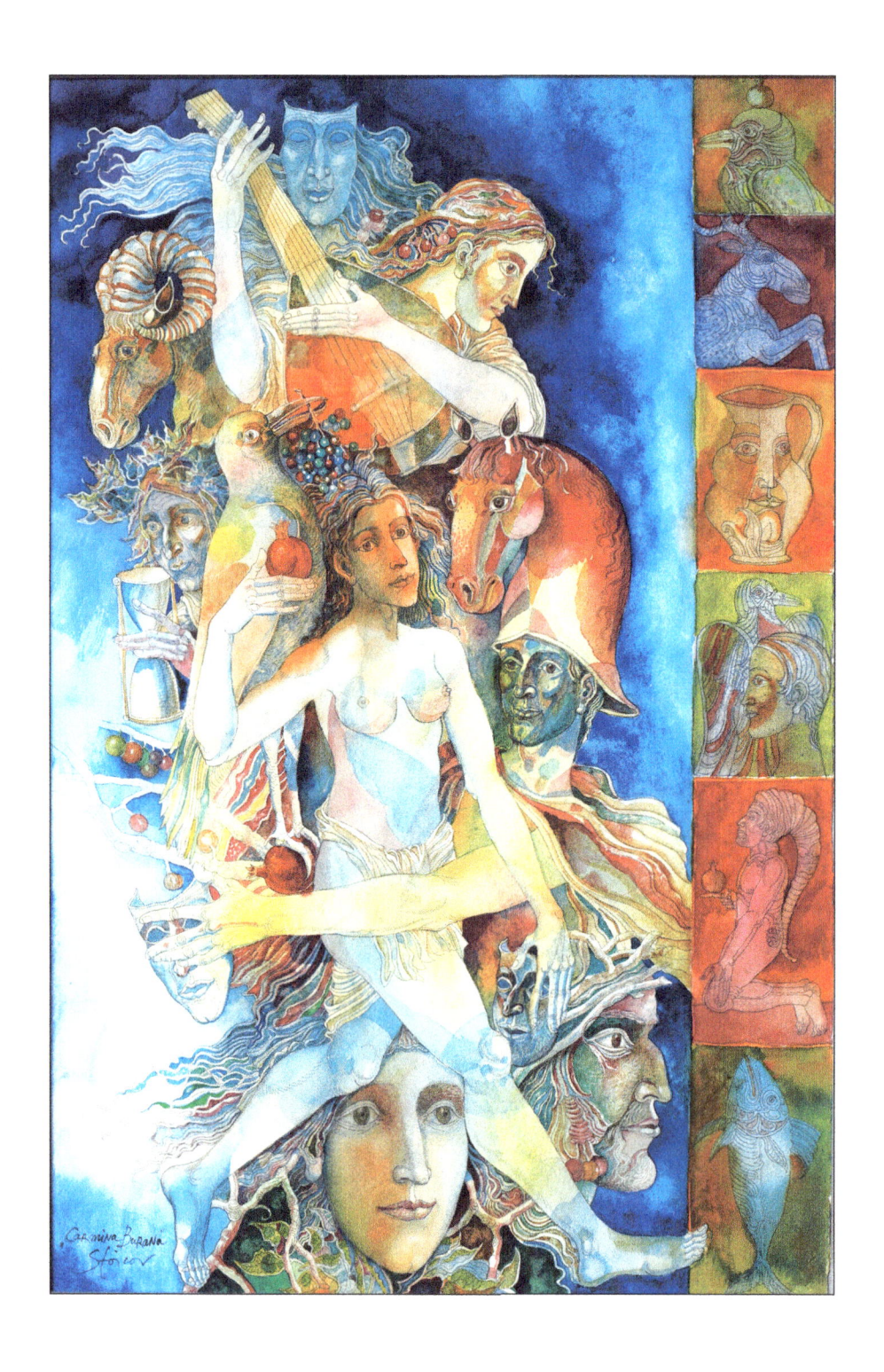

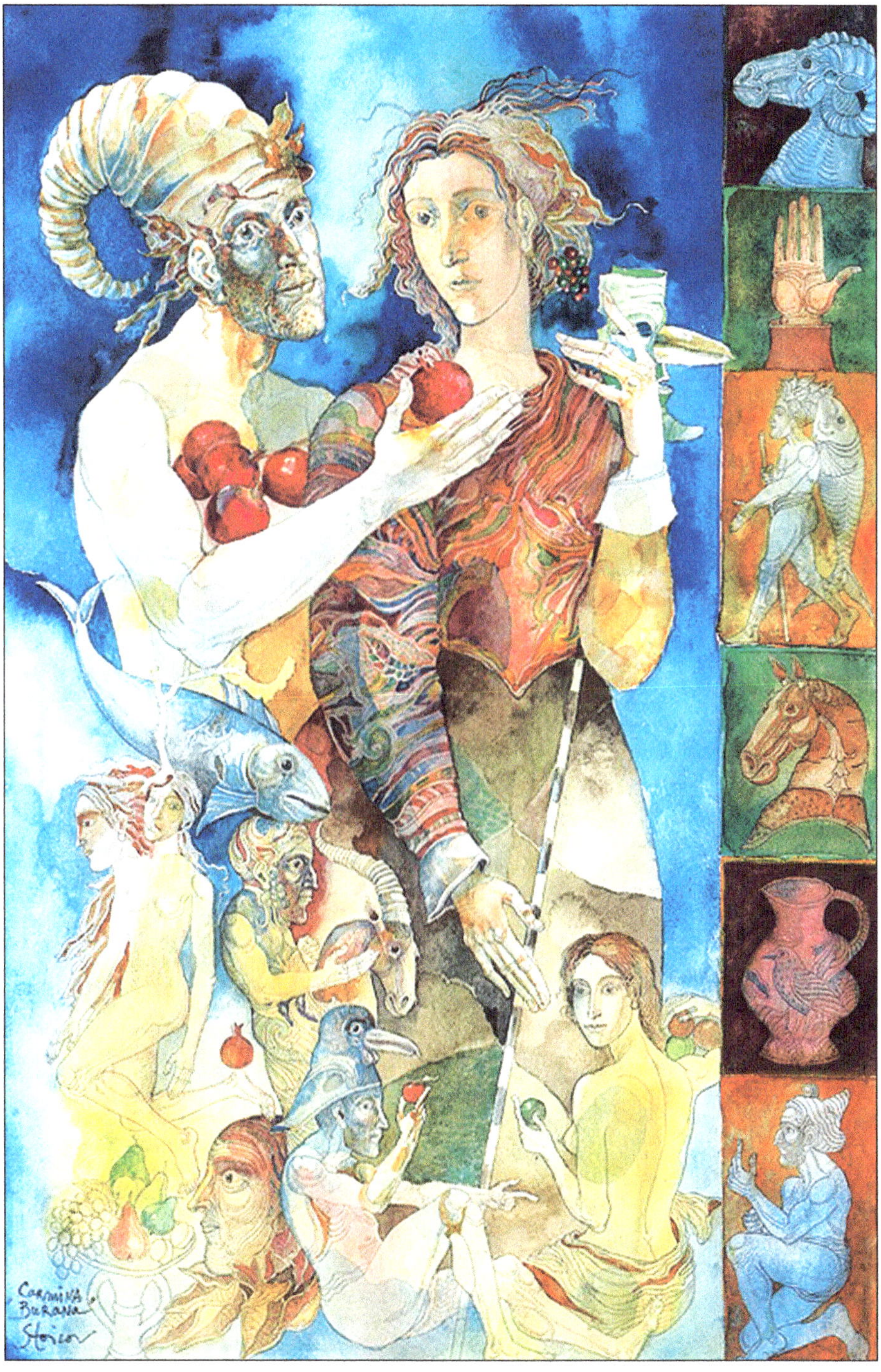
Carmina Burana
Stoica

Green-Winged Horse

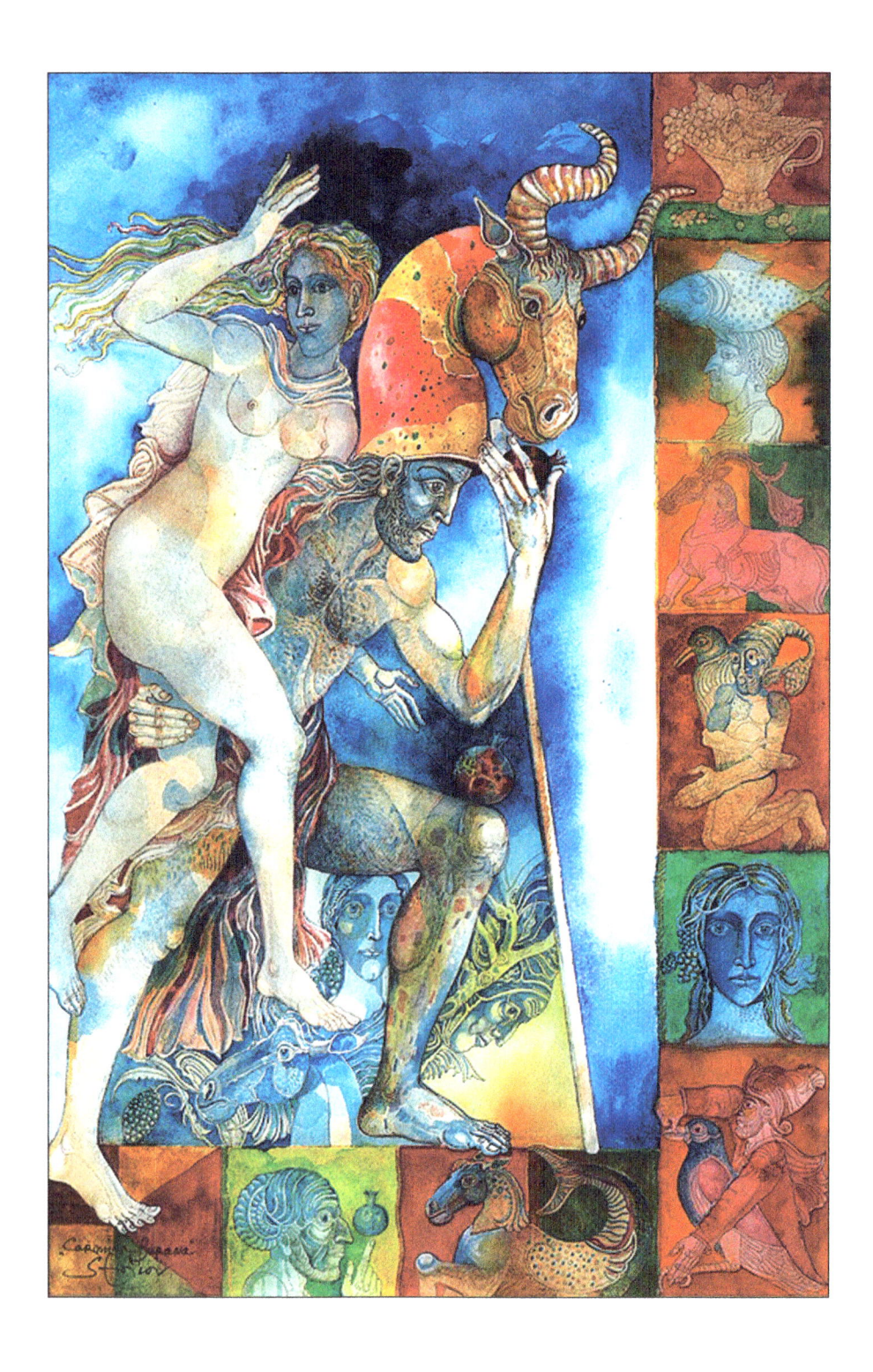

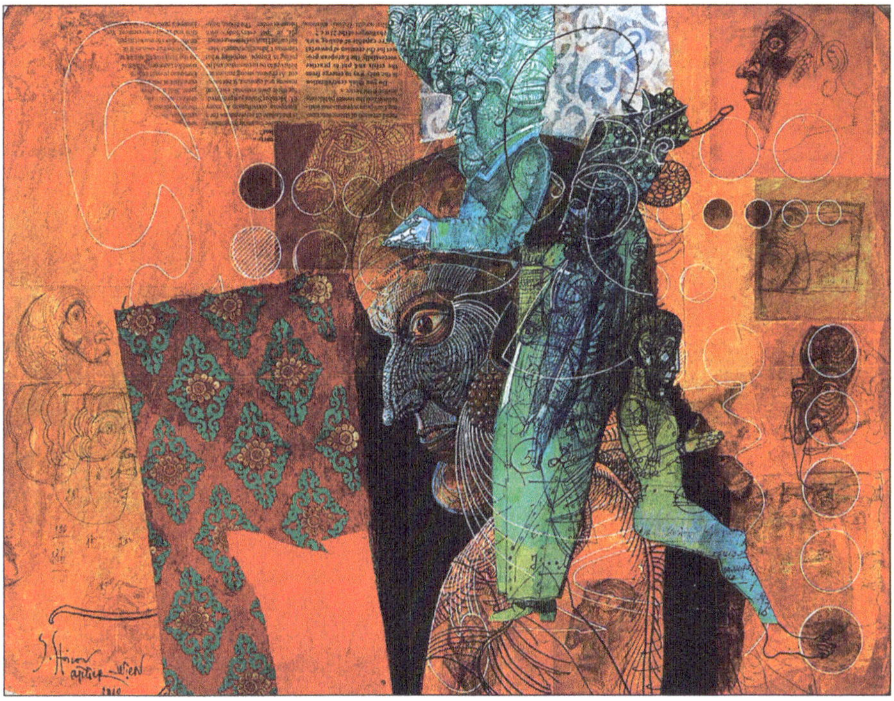

ASHES OF LIGHT

Selected Poems

ASHES OF LIGHT

New and Selected Poems by Lyubomir Levchev

Lyubomir Levchev's poetry craves tranquility and sagacious finality, yet is ruptured by the perplexities of human experience and the vitality of creation. It is apophatic in its assertions, biblical in its axiology, discursive in its rhetoric, and conversational in its method, baring a depth that is both treacherous and soothing. Conceived as the biography of a creator's soul and springing from the well-trodden traditions of neo-romanticism and realism into the realms of ironic skepticism, his poetry is modern and easily read. Behind the soft eloquence and accessible phrase, however, are fierce irony, rigor, and the swift hand of a demiurge with "an aura of violet fatigue" holding tightly the reins of expression. Yet it is difficult to explore the many metastases of his heavy-rooted, omniscient "I" without exploring the shafts of his language. Such an archaeological work will reveal painful self-scrutiny and an ambivalent Sphynxian (Levchev means 'lion's' in Bulgarian) blend of the creative urge and the death wish.

> [...]
> Then we'll sit down at the café
> under the umbrellas on the sidewalk.
> Then we will free ourselves of the secrets.
> A lot of people will go by
> Disgusted with history.
> They will look at me
> with sympathy
> And whisper to themselves: Look at that one—
> Talking with himself without a cell phone.
> Then I'll lean on the edge
> where everything else begins.
> And I'll only feel how love and freedom
> merge within me."
>   "Caprice No. 16"

With Lyubomir Levchev's *Ashes of Light. New and Selected Poems*, Curbstone Press makes a gracious nod to a literature virtually unknown to the American readership. It is a quintessential collection for the eminent Bulgarian poet who has been penning verses for the last 50 years. His latest book of the same title, *Ashes of Light*, published in 2005 and coinciding with the poet's 70th anniversary, comprises poems written in the new century that are by far the most philosophical and dense in his oeuvre. Curbstone's *Ashes of Light* adds to these a handful of earlier poems, tracing the evolution of the poet's imagery, ethos, and form over five decades. The sensuous, almost surreal artwork by Mark McKee augments the feeling of out-of-this-world purposefulness.

Much of the success of this delightful poetry collection is owed to the superb translations from the Bulgarian by Valentin Krustev and Jack Harte, who beautifully capture and convey into English the silences and exultations of the author's unique and highly ironic language.

Lyubomir Levchev belongs to a generation of very talented Bulgarian poets who were ushered into the forefronts of Bulgarian culture after 1956, the year of de-Stalinization in communist Eastern Europe. As the regime transitioned into its more mature post-radical stage, its ideologists, although never retracting from the policy of interning its opponents into socialist-style concentration camps, allowed for a relative liberalization of the rigid Socialist realism canon. Poetry was called on to become the ultimate vehicle of its "humanizing" message. Poets were awarded the romantic aura of elevated human beings chosen to lead the masses to a better brighter future. Out of that thaw came some of the best modernist verse. In a way, the Bulgarian artistic generation of the 50s and 60s did for the Bulgarian literature what the *beatniks* did for America – introduced poetry-for-performance, experimentation with form, internalization of the world's sorrow with a powerful ironic twist of the brush, a quest for the universal truth through allegories, metaphors and obsessive attention to the self and to minuteness.

As one of the most charismatic of this generation, Levchev went on to make a head-spinning career within the communist party and its artistic wing, which inescapably drew clouds of controversy and backlash upon him after communism was officially abolished in Bulgaria in 1989. Some of his later works' preoccupation with duality, marginality, fractured identity, death and freedom as abandonment bear traces of apologetics that one inadvertently reads through the lenses of the author's real-life dialogues with his critics:

> "[...] I am the one-eyed one!"
> the smoke will utter, rising,
> abandoning the fire
> (just as my truest little comrades
> abandoned me) [...]"

("A Tale from 24 451 Nights")

> "[...] I never was as free as now – a beast
> Having escaped from the political zoo.
> So what if across the bridge with its arches of stars
> Some new century is said to have passed.
> [...]
> Lord, thank you for forgetting
> To lock my cage."

("The Gardens of Eternity")

Interestingly, a dispassionate look at some of his earlier poems reveals smug irreverence to the dogmas of the socialist realism as well as a foreboding of the playful concomitance of high- and low-brow notions and language, a matter-of-fact stringing of self-excluding characterizations, and always, everywhere a powerful undercurrent of irony that is the poet's most distinctive trait. "Skepticism is in style again," he writes later on. The anecdote, the smirk, the humorous self-chiding, the vulgarization of speech in fictitious dialogues, the mannerisms, the sardonic comments even, often contextualize the poetic message to the point where cutting just a slice makes quoting anti-climactic. His poetry is like a string of beads, or a rosary– a holistic sequence of simple words held together by deep understanding of the world and the self.

In 1968, he wrote "Poetry Readings," a stand-off between the idea of poetry-read-in-stadiums ("And Zhenya Evtushenko gives readings in stadiums!") and the romantic notion of poetry-read-in sacred hours "like love letters! Like secret leaflets," alluding in earnest to the propaganda leaflets. The poem is a travelogue of poets' visits to "those distant small towns" where in "Canteen No. 2, amid the smell of stew" under the "electric flower of the construction site" they address the 20th century and promise ravishing miracles to the "handful of fitters" who prefer to go out for a smoke.

> [...] Poets can survive everything-
> being hungry,
> and yet sing,
> expelled students…
> But my God,
>   can one possibly do without applause?
> Grin a bit!
> Say it doesn't matter.
> Defeat!
> Defeat! [...]

Pathos and subdued tonality sharply fluctuate through the patchwork of romantically extolling, declaratively realistic and colloquial de-emphasized speech. In the decorated with optimistic exuberance final scene, the poet plays a Hamletian middle-of-the-night monologue in a stadium with "three billion stars sitting on the bleachers." And he recites to them "how man rises./ And how difficult it is for him to shine all life long. Yet with his own light/ reduces himself to ashes/over new foundations/or over honest stanzas…" How man rises and turns to ashes is Levchev's retort to "to be or not to be" in the wholesale vision of the stadium as a grandiose locus of the collective soul, quite in tune with the 1960s, the times of the industrialization and space exploration in communist Eastern Europe. A time when love happened under the power plant chimney stack or on a bridge with locomotives rattling underneath amid clouds and steam.

Rigor and bold declarative statements chimed well in the context of the socialist writing. That type of poetry freely borrowed devices from the expressionist movement embraced by the Bulgarian poets of the 1920s and 1930s. The language is expressive and the statements direct. The poet's mind cannot stand still, it is not even simply searching, rather it is in a state of entropy, growing, permeating, engulfing vast expanses of space and universe, much like Whitman or Ginsberg. Only time remains out of reach, at least for the young Levchev. To the extent that this is a vision akin to romanticism, romanticism plays just a procedural role in his method, similar to the rhetorical questions used to trigger a key change of logic or direction in the discourse. Over the years, the poet has filtered the brazenness of youth, and his verse, no less expressive and just as wise and witty, starts to exhibit a quality of modulation intrinsic to the complicated spiritual life of a modern tragic man.

The program poem, "Ashes of Light," written in 2005, picks up the metaphor from 1968 as well the construction symbolism. House-building reverberates through several of his poems as a symbol of creativity and life:

> I have found a house
> older than the Universe.
> And master-builders turned up right away.
> Well, you've bought
> quite an old elephant there,
> they said.
> Actually old age is irremediable.
> Better to pull it down
> and make
> something entirely new
> out of the material."
> [...]
> Be wary of the master-builders
> who offer
> to repair the world

In between the nimble irony of the opening lines and the didactic presentiment of the ending, self-isolationist sentiments sound off against a backdrop of purely symbolist imagery. The protagonist is cloistered in a room behind glass walls "like a wick burning low./Ashes of Light," ruminating about the sunset, another favorite allegory of old age in Levchev's cosmology, that nestles in him at night and tiptoes away in the morning. The stars of his youth have mutated into enormous moths with crimson eyes. The foundations of the house-world are hiding the caravan of time full of secrets. Sometime over the years "how man rises" has become irrelevant and is duly replaced by "And I pretend that I don't hear." The poetry of ecstasy has morphed into the poetry of Nirvana.

This is one of the very few poems where the poetic Self dissolves into the practice of quiet meditation, and no desires or fears tempt the imagination. The didactic ending thus reads as a philosophical commentary on a world in which the line between good and evil has thinned out and become ineffable. Hence the abundance of characters of marginal status but grand axiological value for the human experience: the poet, the visionary, the naked idol, the madman, the traveler or ancient god, the artist, the old man…Likewise, Levchev is preoccupied with the borderline dots on the temporal axis. Time is the one most troubling metaphysical notion for the poet. In 1968, he writes the exquisite farcical poem "Caprice No. 1," where in a delightfully paradoxical verse his persona appoints Death as his secretary and listens in on Death's refutations to the people calling in that "he is definitely not here," and all the while through that infinite time he is gazing out the window at the world's routine involving, among other things, changes of seasons and girls looking at themselves in glass doors. Time in 2005, however, is a formidable unforgiving anti-thesis of the forgiving God. It "hides the treasure of virgin happiness," yet is unattainable: either go stolen, irretrievable or has never begun. "Do you know what it is like to be and yet be unable to make a start," a young character in "Lullaby" channels Hamlet's philosophical question. Time can just stop, "a scarecrow sees how the infinitive tense appears, how the shade of time sways and halts abruptly." The poet's present time is "a withered posy left without water." The most profound articulation of the myth of creation and dialectics of life presents itself in "Spiderman:"

> […] There is a time for making nests,
> the Preacher will say.
> Then God provides
> his special mud.
> Nature provides the straw.
> We-labor.
> And here comes history
> and lays its cuckoo's eggs
> in us.
> Man, possessed of history,
> wants to fly away from himself.
> He flaps the wings
> he doesn't have.
> He is great, if he perishes.
> He is wretched if he survives.
> For it's not him but history that flies off.
> Then he climbs down
> his thin posthistoric threat
> into the nothingness.
> Into ordinary time,
> which has neither cause,
> nor consequence.[…]

Throughout the book, internalized biblical imagery provides the framework for expressing the soul's existential drama. The mythological illumination in Levchev's poetry draws its power from the heroic narratives, possessing high symbolic status in the Bulgarian poetic tradition. Mythological versus ordinary time, freedom versus abandonment, the solitary visionary-poet-madman versus his disillusioned wretched memoir-writing inconsequential imitation. The biography of the soul unravels a spiritual journey towards ridding the soul of time, words, and experiences in pursuit of a Sartrean freedom that is so emptied of human breath and worldly passions that looks almost utopian. The other condition as an end-in-itself is love when "I'll forget your name./ I'll forget to breathe./ And only your tenderness will flow instead of time" ("Letter"). Levchev's love poems are masterful creations of intellectual intensity and emotional drama.

On a larger scale, paramount to Borges's vision of a universal ever-living library, the principle of dictionary provides the Bulgarian poet with a method to fathom and narrate the state of being. A dictionary is a collection of all words, signifiers of both literal and abstract meanings, tied to each other by phonetic proximity. Stunning paradoxes, parallels and lightning metaphors produce the thrust in Levchev's poems. He alights on a word's adjacent associative nest, either through proximity or argument, and assure the conversational flow, whether quiet or theatrical, often infusing the text with a thought's elliptical motion within a structured hierarchy:

> I am walking.
> And I am leading my father by the hand.
> And he is ever smaller and smaller.
> He has lost the key to home.
> But he will never admit it.
> Like son, like father.
> And actually now
> I don't know where I could take him.
> The Internet café
> is closed for prophylaxis.
> Besides,
> I don't know
> how to open the site
> to the Hereafter.
> I only know
> that the world is a sentence
> from a long apocrypha for gods.
> And I am trying
> to build up a home of words.
> But it collapses on me.
> And I shout
> oxygen,

help me burn down more quickly!
I feel intolerably wretched!
Iron,
I renounce you!
Damn you,
rigidness.
The world is a manner of expression.
Daddy,
I don't want to be a father!
I feel terribly wretched.
Mom,
I don't want to become older than you, either! [...]
              "The Last Caprice"

As is often the case, Levchev directly summons up or metonymically points to these hierarchies and ultimate meanings. In "Ultima Verba" he expands on the word/world relation, "...this world is made/ of the ultimate words/of other worlds. Quite other. Quite vanished.../ And then I feel/ I'm one of them." Whether he is the word or the world is not clear – and most probably he is both. Because the otherness and the act of vanishing seem to most often ignite the creative energies in this book.

In "The Wall," Levchev appeals to the eyes not to say goodbye to the visible world because he feels like a manuscript that "has already been written down/ but not yet read." As with most everything in this very entertaining, shockingly direct, intellectually provoking, existentially powerful poetry, the vector of transcendence is neutralized by the vector of jest: "Now I feel so bookish / that I am writing on my own self—/ unrepentant and/ with unsharpened lightings." ("Irish Fantasies").

If, reading this book, you, reader, are stricken by an unsharpened lightning, then the Bulgarian poet must be holding you by the hand on a journey "out of the wicked words." But beware, although he promises freedom and sublimation, he may be joking...

Zoya Marincheva

A native of Bulgaria, Zoya Marincheva has made Texas her second home for 13 years. Her academic background is in Bulgarian Philology and English, and her curiosity in global affairs has driven her to occasional forays into economics and law.

A poet, blogger, journalist and literary translator, she is determined to make Bulgarian voices heard in the world.

Her translations and original work in English and Bulgarian have appeared in To Topos (Univ. of Oregon), Two Lines, Washington Square Review (NYU), Montreal Review, Zoland Poetry, Evergreen Review, Liternet, Crosspoint, Dictum, etc. *Most recently, her collaborative digital poetry,* Illuminations, *was selected and featured in the 2012 editions of the prestigious art festivals Luminaria, Texas, and Sofia Poetics, Bulgaria.*

GIMMEBREADYE

My friend, what makes you sad?...
You look so wretched today.
Take a cigarette.
Let's have a smoke…

The smoke is growing like a tree
bearing dreams.
And its fruit is ripe,
and sweet, and bitter.

Listen, if you want I can tell you
about Gimmebreadye…
The snow is falling, falling,
as if it wants to cover up the dark,
while the dark keeps gushing
from beneath the drift,
and the wind, the wind whistles…

The homeless kid's
little feet come to a halt
in front of our door.
And through the iron keyhole,
a frozen voice implores:
"Gimmebreadye!…"

He's my age, goes barefoot.
He carries wood and coal
to earn some bread.
That's why they call him Gimmebreadye…

And off he goes carrying the huge buckets.
I follow him with the key to open up the basement—
and then Mom stops me at the door:
"Watch out he doesn't swipe something down there!…"
Going down the staircase I wonder:
what could he swipe?
Both his hands are busy
with the buckets, right?...

Yet the great thief
swiped my heart!…

A pure smile:
"Do you know how to smoke?"

And we are buddies now
smoking from the same cigarette.
And I am choking from the smoke
and listening, listening…
as if I were the single soldier
of that fairytale country
where he's the great king, and
his throne the upturned bucket.

I study that courageous profile
and listen to his lofty words,
how one day he'll hit the road
and catch up with the circus,
how he'll become a famous clown
with a hump back and a cardboard
nose in the bright arena…
And he will let me in for free…

Gimmebreadye, the poorest on earth,
is sitting on his throne, and everyone's
so small before his laughter…
And the entire earth
is but a grain of wheat.

My friend, when I feel wretched
and failures whip my heart,
and my days on earth start tasting
bitter, and I feel like crying,
an enormous clown stands up
with a hump back and a cardboard nose…
And laughs, and laughs, that clown,
when I am crying!

CONTINUOUS POEM

Many nights before the
birth of our great intimacy
we would meet like glances.

– And what are you thinking of now?...

We would meet like lips:

– And what are you thinking of now?...

One evening, suddenly,
we began to read
each other's thoughts.
We smiled simultaneously.
Quite simply – we set forth.

My embrace shielded you
from the fierce rain, and we
turned golden in the shop windows.
The sidewalks reflected us.

The drivers in the street scolded us.
Mothers with many children laughed at us.
And all our former lovers
were serenading us
on distant trumpets.

We were flying
and we asked
the shadows,
the winds,
the stars,
the drain pipes
and the phone booths
a spot for two lovers.

In the Library Park.

"A spot for two lovers!"

Under the smokestacks at
the Maritza power plant.

"A spot for two lovers!"
On the Bourgas seawall.

"A spot for two lovers!"
How small our Earth is!

"A spot for two lovers!"

How short our days are!

How long will we have to fly
looking for a spot for two lovers?

THE LAND OF THE MURDERED POETS

Between the Arctic Circle
and the Tropic of Cancer
(between passion and thought)
and so far from heaven, a land
is burgeoning, beautiful and
abundant, the land
of the murdered poets…

Yet poems emerge and well up dark.
They tear me to pieces. And behold,
as in old, the woman reaper cuts
a swath of sunny rays.
"But you're alive!" The eagle takes offense.
The wolf's eyes search for my wounds.

A land for me! A land deep within me!
You call from hours bereft of sleep.
And the mad Maritza river of my blood
is eating away the banks of my heart.
And I am learning to write down verses
in the land of the murdered poets.

WE STOPPED

We stopped right under
the sign, "No stopping!"
And then you said to me:
"This is my favorite spot."

A bridge of rails and planks.
Oh, rusty rainbow! And a sign:
"No stopping!"

Yet, no river flows beneath
the bridge. Railroads flow there.
And flagmen wave their wings.
And the midnight shunting groan.

And when the locomotives rattled
under our feet, clouds of steam
enveloped us. Totally invisible,
and totally alone, we kissed each other.

Perhaps there are millions of cars
loaded with our kisses sent out
far and wide across the world.
We were about to leave,
when I said to you:
"This is my favorite spot."

A bridge. Magical. And unforgettable.
Between childhood and adulthood.
And a sign, "No stopping!"

MORNING

Yes, the dark wind is full of
the clanging of alarm clocks.
Hurry up, my boy!
Yes, the milkmaid is delivering the
morning in jars and in plastic cups.
Hurry up! They'll turn us away!
Yes, our mouths are breathing clouds.
Yes, we look like dragons. One of us
big, and the other one—smaller
and not yet quite awake…
Hurry up! At the kindergarten door
the little dragon lets go of my hand:
"And can you for once come
and pick me up first,
while all the dolls are crying 'mama'
and all the hobbyhorses gallop
but aren't heading home.
Can you?" "I'll try, my dragon child."

I can summon the past.
I can see into the future.
I can crush with verse
my most malicious foes.
And I tell death that I'm a man.
But could I just for once…

Yes, the dark wind is full of
the clanging of alarm clocks.
And the dark wind is me.
And fathers are awakening in me.

How odd, one of my hands
is warm, the other – cold.

AND HERE I AM

To Bistra

And look: here I am again waiting
for the great love to come.
And look: here I am looking again
at the large clock. On the big hand
a dove has perched, alone like me.
Red clouds fume in the afternoon
silence. And look: the clock ticks,
and the big hand drops down a notch.
The dove's wings explode.
The frightened bird flies off
like an Egyptian soul.
I watch above the rooftops
a lost minute flitting
and disappearing.
And the dove's fear
rests in my heart.

DÉNOUEMENT

You are undressing as if for the doctor.

Such thought fractures in my mind.
And suddenly everything turns fragile.
The little vase becomes a test tube,
and the flower—some strange bacillus.
And you laugh aloud at me:
"Come on, come on!
Ask me how I'm feeling.
And what my trouble is.
And where it hurts...
Ask whatever you want!
Just don't pretend."

And I bend down mechanically.
"Take a deep breath," I say.

And the air takes you deeply in.

And you disappear.
You're no longer here.
The bed still clasps your warmth—
the torn clothes of a fugitive.
But you've broken loose.
Forever.

Most likely you are now
descending down memory.
You're crying, and the
zipper of your skirt is torn.
And your voice is broken.

I hear: Goodbye,
       darling,
            goodbye!"

Goodbye, my desired one!
I wish you all the best,
and some of the pain.

CAPRICE NO. 1

If I should have a career someday
(and they maintain it is inevitable),
if I should rise so high that they start
phoning me from everywhere, then
I will appoint death as my secretary.

And when you phone and ask for me,
she'll say that I'm not in.
"But perhaps just for a moment…"
"No!" she'll say, "He is definitely not here!"
And all the while through that infinite time
I'll be gazing out the window
at how the leaves are falling,
or turning green, at how the distant
church dome resembles a demitasse,
turned upright for telling fortunes,
at how the girls look at themselves in glass doors,
and how you are thinking that I am entirely gone.

CAPRICE NO. 2

Dammit! This world is so mercurial,
so entertaining, and so kind
that it begins to remind me
of a hanged man's house.

And I am giggling.
I am wandering the streets
with some friend of mine
who figures out the cunning game
to look at the women first in the face
and then guess what their legs are like.
And I am giggling.

We go on playing,
each one on his own account.
And I am giggling…

Yet how I feel like talking about the rope!
Ah, how I feel like talking about the rope!…

CAPRICE NO. 3

I.
You.
The blank walls.
The night everywhere.
The windows filled with
Whiskey, a girl's warmth.

You.
The wind.
The fantasy of the stars.
The falling of a leaf upon the asphalt.
The wind....

Oh, split second, stop!
        Look!
        Listen!
        And then go.

Unless Doctor Faustus is coming—
having found an excuse for everything.

POETRY READING

Poetry readings, poetry readings...!
From he small students' clubs
to the triumphal halls, against
windmills, and against ghosts,
in dreadful working days
yet without chain armor,
the poet follows his poetry all life long,
Sancho Panza following his Don Quixote.

Well, of course, each has
received his bouquet of flowers.

But there are those distant small towns!
A railway stop. Dogs barking.
Mounds of beets and empty crates...
And look, we slowly
fall out of the evening train.

And beneath the little signal-bell
that ill-at-ease kid our eternal
and unknown brother in the art awaits,
calling us like spirits into his world.

Always "on behalf of all the
enthusiastic construction workers,"
said to be "lovers of poetry readings"...

All right! We set off as silent as a patrol.
The shortcut resembles a field.

But ahead of us like heroin
The electric flower of the
construction site shines excitedly.
And in Canteen Number 2,
amid the smell of stew,
we are addressing you,
twentieth century:

> "You are blood-stained
> with dreams
> and delusions!
> You need
>   crazy poets...!"

"We will sweep your heavens free of mines...!"

Ah, we are promising ravishing miracles.
But the handful of pipe fitters
who have come to hear us,
aren't enchanted. They go out for a smoke.
Sheer bewilderment shines blue in their eyes:
"What are these artists stirring us for…?"

Poets can survive anything –
being hungry, and yet sing,
being unemployed, expelled students...
But, my God, can one of them
possibly do without applause?
Grin a bit! Say it doesn't matter.
But a hole will appear in your soul—
Defeat! Defeat!

And so, how often in dining cars
we would wash away our wounds
with brandy, and someone would sigh
with tragic irony:
"And Yevgeny Yevtushenko
gives readings in football stadiums!
That's how it is with Russians, my friend—
they listen to you, even if you're not that great...
And even when they don't understand a thing,
still in some place like New York,
they will applaud you..."

"Oh, no! Stadiums are not for poems!
Poems are read in sacred hours,
like love letters, like secret leaflets
which require not demonstrations,
but dedication…!"

But the return train would stop
and the poets would disperse
to their old lodgings,
to their new battlefields…

Along the park, along the stadium,
I, too, happened to be returning late…
when all of a sudden I spotted
that the fence was ripped down.
And a smile dawned on me.
And like a thought from the past
I passed through it and past the
deserted bleachers to the immense crater.

A discarded bottle
clattered down the steps,
like an absurd bell
in an absurd amphitheater.

And then, then I was overtaken
by that romantic adventure.
Three billion stars were sitting
in the bleachers, all staring at me.
And I began to recite
in a surprising voice.
And my sincerest passions
echoed selflessly in the dark.
I think was telling the stars
how man rises. And how difficult
it is for him to shine all life long.
Yet with his own light,
reduced himself to ashes
over new foundations
or over honest stanzas…

If there had been a watchman,
he'd have thought me crazy.
But you know I couldn't care less.

My poetry reading was so real,
I permit you to envy me!

CAPRICE No. 6

It's true that I am overburdened.
It's true that I carry a cargo of memories.
It's true that some are forbidden and dangerous…

I'm sailing with a list like some doomed ship.
"We'll sink!"—
the captain shouts from within.
"It's possible, I say,
    "but I won't jettison anything."

"The first big wave will send us down
to dine with the girls from Atlantis!"
"Well, okay, okay…"
I'll try not to worry too much.

And isn't it obvious that I am calm?

I cross the "Sound of Sweet Fatigue."
I heave to in the "Bay of Whispers."
Your hand is burning in my hand
like a covered lantern.

The park swings are rocking on their own,
like in the old days
when I was invisible.

And only their metallic exclamation is heard,
or the grating of armor
from some saga
or from some somber ballad…

There my youth is calling:
Love,
how much you have given me!
Love,
how much you have taken from me!

But today I don't need your words!
I only need your voice.
I throw myself into it.
I hide my head as in my mother's lap.
I wriggle happily.

I'm sinking,
ever deeper,
ever deeper.
To where girls from Atlantis
bring me amphorae of fragrant madness.

CAPRICE No. 7

I drank of insincere feelings.
I drank because I was dying of thirst,
	because I was parched,
	because I was already cracking.
I drank of insincere feelings—
deceptive,
sticky,
sweet swift-flowing transience!

I drank, and now I feel sick.
In the West the sunset is painting
a portrait of my absence.
The bells are ringing.
The Lord is also drinking.
And in my eyes are snow-covered expanses...

Oh how I hope my face won't betray me!
I offer my entire kingdom
for just one smile!
Why didn't I die of thirst!

CAPRICE No. 11

The Sacred Volcano –
that woodcut, carved with
a few scratches by Hokusai,
shines in my mind
more powerful than reality
and far more true than nature.

For the real mountain,
the real Fujiyama,
it's so improbable
I could accept it only
as a dream, as a sigh,
an interjection. Ah...

Its foot is lost in a mist of
tenderness. Only its snow-capped
crown gleams in the sky like a
phantom, like a balcony, but one
that projects from the void of
the universe from the castle
of the unknown.

I wouldn't believe my eyes
if I didn't know that
such a celestial balcony floats
incredible in me.
Once in a few million years
you step out on it, my love.
You step out to see if there are any stars.
But instead you discover
the murderous dark man.

I love you!
This whisper at the very end,
this final word, having thrown out
all its meaning so it can carry
all its feeling. I love you!

No. That's no word.
That surely is the ultimate particle
that is left of me. The ultimate
real something that I have.
Take it!

THE GARDEN BEFORE PARADISE

For Radoy Rallin

The Field Marshal went by.
He didn't like the town.
The tanks went by.
The trucks went by.
And only a bumpy road remained.
And a hundred injured horses.

A sentimental commander
had made a strange gesture—
he had given a team of horses
freedom and peace…
and this during wartime hunger.

These were not graceful circus actors
nor slender-legged steeplechase jumpers.
These were warhorses, made deaf by guns,
blind by fire, horses with spotless honor.

Decorated with monstrous wounds,
they grazed slowly in an orchard,
and drank long from the stone trough
their last sacrament before going
to Paradise.

No one shod them anymore. Only
the nightingales sang their evening praises.
Only one very old soldier was detailed to
take care of them and like them finish his life.
His entire family had been killed long before.
All of them were buried in his absence.
And now he buried the horses like a centaur.
He would fire once in the air
and make the sign of the cross.

There he is in front of the straw hut,
well-groomed, with all his medals and insignia,
having passed through all the bloody dramas
and having hidden all his pain beneath a simple pride.

We, the children, used to bring him cigarettes
and matches, which we'd swipe from our fathers and brothers.
But he would accept no presents, so we'd leave them
there beside him, on the grass.

He recognized our passion for riding,
our passion for the frightening.
our passion for what was forbidden...
And with a simple nod of his head,
he would point at the horses allotted to us.

The wounded horses would give us a gentle lick
while we climbed up barefoot by their manes.
And they would set forth heavily—
with a warlike gait, they—for the last time—
we—for the first time— happy.

We lived long, but we did not grow old
and they did not kill us. And now when I hear
that Shiva is dancing again,
I hear my heart howl distantly and quietly.
"Captain, it's useless to undergo any treatment!
Our flesh isn't even good for horse-sausages.
And if we survive this last battle till the end,
make your strange and dangerous gesture—
let us in to die in the garden before Paradise."

LETTER

Poste Restante

The red luminary takes leave.
The last wild lynx peers into
what's invisible to us.
The snow on the summits takes leave.
The motionless lift-cabins
travel on towards oblivion,
travel on. Like a dream driven
away. Like a desperate hope.
The epoch takes leave.
Ecstasy takes leave.
And it seems only I am left.

I don't know if I'll be able to write to you again.
I don't know if I'll be able to see you.
But I know there is no way I could forget you
until the end and maybe even after that.

I'll leave my keys in the door of nonexistence.
I'll leave my glasses and go blind.
I'll be looking for you with bleeding fingers
but everything I touch will burn to ashes.
I'll forget your name. I'll forget to breathe.
And only your tenderness will flow instead of time.
And only your whisper in the ear of darkness…

Ok. I heard.
Goodbye!
Goodbye!
Goodbye!
Goodbye!

At which slave market did you buy me
and leave me, before you set me free?
What is it that I hold tight in my sunken heart?
Even if I knew I would no longer tell you.

LOVE IN THE MILITARY HOSPITAL

or Homage to the Great French Revolution

Night's greatcoat is large for us – It will
cover us both and still trail on the ground.
It will cover our tracks and just
our words will remain to wander about
and find each other sometimes.

It so happens I've bid farewell to arms,
yet in such a way that God will remember me.
But I have never been in any military hospital.

By the quiet, poisonous Don
I have rolled, slain by
a Cossack girl's eyelashes.
But I have never been
in any military hospital.

Among stars and sand and plague
with the dreadful artist Gros
I have contemplated the visit
of the great mirages.
But I have never...
Yet, yesterday
we were in the military infirmary.
Covered by the greatcoat –
like a puddle among puddles
of clotted and blood yet to be shed.
Among piles of pus-stained bandages
and gauze and heavy metal chains
we lay embraced, no, clung to one another.
You had stopped my fatal wound with a kiss
and my soul was flowing out not into chaos
and the pitch dark but into you, my light abyss.

At the bottom. That's where I wished to hide myself.
We were trembling, both of us. While around us
the blind, the amputated, the drugged, the doomed
were screaming, were vomiting death screams:
"Allons enfants! Allons enfants!"
"Égalité!" "Fraternité!"

The sailor with the amputated legs
broke into a song with his last inspiration:

"Rot Front!" – the armless raised his arms.
"Avanti popolo!" "¡No Pasarán!"
"Za Stalina, za Rodinu!"
"Za Stalina! ..." – the punitive squad was shouting,
as well as those – the others, the half buried
in the thirty million graves ones.
"¡Patria o muerte!" "¡Venceremos!"

And maybe I am also already blind.
And that's why I am caressing you like mad.
I read you like Braille: "Forgive me!"
And you whisper: "Not that! Say that other thing!
Say it to me again!"And I shout, "I love you!"
like someone just convicted, the way
one cries out his last words.

Don't worry, they won't hear us
in the twentieth-century military
infirmary among all these screams,
moans, curses, wheezes, and residual silence.

When the grave diggers come for me
tomorrow morning say you've already burned me.
Say that's what I wanted – to be burned separately.
Don't say that you mean your fire.
As for my name, it may stay with the others
in the common grave. But even that's too much.
Better claim until the end that I have never
been in any military hospital.

I WHO DID NOT FLEE POMPEII

Death is a mystery. A fear. But hardly an end.
Earth's cradle rocks me in the void.
And I hear the spheres—the crystal-clear signals—
I who did not flee Pompeii.

Before the excavations brought me forth
curled like an embryo, silent, petrified—
I simply withstood the brunt of the elements.
And the perishable clung to me.

I watched you running down the slope
toward boats and lifesaving lies.
Having robbed the temples, you prayed
your sin was blamed on someone else.

Men. Beasts… Everything vanished.
How beautiful Pompeii the waste was!
A few blades of grass stayed with me.
And glory crept up slowly like a villain.

God was replaced. They studied the Volcano.
The corrupt city has become a museum.
And only I remained here with myself,
I who did not flee Pompeii.

TOMORROW'S BREAD

Once I reproached my son
because he did not know
where to buy bread.
And now...
he is selling bread
in America.
In Washington.
In his daytime routine
he teaches at the university.
At night he writes poetry.
But on Saturdays and Sundays
he sells bread on the
corner of Nebraska and Connecticut.

The fields of Bulgaria are empty.
Those women of the earth who used to
reap the crops to feed the generations,
are fading away like the notes of a dying song.
Politicians set up their melodrama:
"Who filched the wheat of the motherland?!"
But what lies between bread and man remains
hidden behind the several names,
different in taste and different in price.

My son sells bread for sandwiches,
rosemary buns, olive rolls,
"Zaatar" loaves, Spanish sesame "Semolina,"
walnut bread, wheat bread, sprinkled with raisins,
Italian "Pane Bello."
"Palladin," kneaded with olive oil, with yeast and milk,
corn bread, pumpkin-seed bread,
Turkish bread, bread made of clouds…
Only Bulgarian bread is not available,
nor the leftover bread from yesterday!

"Some bread remains unsold
every day," my son says.
"We are given a loaf for dinner.
The rest is wrapped in plastic bags
and dumped…"
Weariness weighs on my son.
The bread has handed him an American dream
(And this, too, means The American Dream)!
Oh God, don't you hear? My son is praying for something!
Danger encircles him like an aura.

Give me the answer, Lord, to one single prayer -
to one last wish,
then do, please, whatever my son asks of you.
And sure, you might as well adopt him!

In Sofia
the shades of old women
scour the dark.
Ransacking the rubbish bins they collect bread.
Pointing at one of them, a teacher
of history and Bulgarian language, they say:

"Don't jump to conclusions, take it easy!
She's not taking the bread for herself. She feeds
stray dogs and birds."
And my words too are food for dogs
and birds.

Oh God!
Why am I alive?
Why do I wander alone in the Rhodopes?
Why do I gaze down abandoned wells?
Why do I dig into caves where people lie?
And pass the night in sacred places, renounced by you?

I am seeking the way
to the last magician's hideout,
he who forgot to die
but has not forgotten the secret of bread.
Not today's bread, which is for sale,
not yesterday's bread which has been dumped...
I must know the secret of tomorrow's bread.
The bread we kiss in awe.
The bread that takes our children by the hand
and leads them all back home.

LIGHTHOUSE

To N. Bozhilov

Naked as an idol—
banned—
I am lying under palm-tree clouds,
buried alive in the finite sky…

But I'm preoccupied by other things.

Does one live on after it's over?
Or is there some other way of existence?
Or do only invisible traces of us
remain, which even the stellar Dogs
of the celestial Hunter lose?
Or is the astral space filled with souls,
the way my glass is filled with emptied glasses?

What does one do in Paradise?
I want to do something. The Paradise Rock
lies beyond the bend. But before that
I passed the white, solitary universe
where Jules Verne had been drawing up his prophecies.

On the other side of the gulf,
beyond the green mist,
Chagall
had been flying with or without violin...
Only those twisting stone-pines have remained from the song—
the game of azure features—
the game of Nulla dies sine linea.

But thought
scales other slopes.

Paths are quickly overgrown.
Wounds never close.
A different god has triumphed.
Let us hope he will be better.

I have never understood
who was the abandoned one—
me or the ocean.
There I buried the utopia and the compass.

Now I'm lying under the palm trees of Eden Rock.
Silver helicopters and hydroplanes
are humming and entering the flower of the sun.
They keep gathering wisdom,
until the evening settles in
and the discos on the beach
fill up with oblivion like honeycombs .

Then the lighthouse of Garoupe
like a cavalry horse
harnessed to a garden wheel
spins the world's wheel again.

The Moon, a silver ball,
bumps against the stars
and stops again on black!
And skepticism is in style again.

But my thought...

I have not staked it
on either a color or a number.

The human soul boils with love and peril.
The incest of constellations gives birth
to new illusions, new religions, and new apostles.
They are foretold.
They are called "second history."
It's them I count on.
And it's to them I send my signals.

But during the day the lighthouse of Garoupe
is only a pale ghost
southwest of old Antibes.

PIER

good, perhaps, for Noah

On dry land boats become other creatures.
They lie down, deceiving, persuading
themselves they've been hunted by the storm.
In fact, they are out of use.
To flow into moist sand, now that's the
saddest self-foundering for both boats and dreams!
The former already look like flowerpots.
Weeds make love inside them.
The latter are raised up like a fence,
a refuge against the wind.
And coals—black bones—betray the secret
of the fire, where the oars have burned.
Close to the pier a rotted boat
has hauled itself up on tiptoe, hull skyward.
A temple on piles. And within sleeps a traveler
or an ancient god. He has abandoned his rigid
mythology and now sleeps on his stomach,
having turned his back on the skies...
His hand moves.
Perhaps he has hunted the vexing full moon
or else he dreams he has flung
his harpoon towards some nebulous spirit.
Near the jetty, I am watching him, silently.
I'm concerned that if I wake him
he will cry out, having rubbed his eyes:
"There's my image, disfigured by
its education, by morals, by its nurture,
and by its frequent reformation."
He will die of jealousy seeing me freer than he is.
"Not more free, but abandoned," I would cry out
deliberately, no doubt.

He will insist: "Look at my original image."

He knows neither his beginning nor his end.
He doesn't even know that in this world
imitation precedes the image!

CAPRICE NO. 16

Something lies hidden in this not entirely discovered world.

Someone's breath penetrates
my spirit and lurks
behind the curtain of autumn.
Perhaps a fugitive dream waits
for reality to fall asleep. Or perhaps
the condemned sunset had breathed
its last sigh:
– Mother, the dark.

Hey, you, the Invisible one,
if you're a thief
take whatever you want:
Dreams. Illusions. Utopias.
These exquisite fantasies
won't make you rich
in this world of toughs and gangsters.

If you're a killer
you're too late!
The angelic-faced
moral maximalists are already ahead of you.
But what would it cost you
to try again?
Have another go, my friend!
Repetitio mater studiorum est.

If you're homeless, stay!
The bread and wine are on the table.
Lie to them that you're a friend
from the barracks. Or else,
that you are my time.
And you've already come.

But if you are the Messenger,
I am waiting for you.
If you wish to know the secret,
whether silence is deaf-mute,
or pretends to be a dead thunder.
you should first recognize me.

In the mazes of the secret monster
or in Madame Tussaud's museum,

one hundred sorcerers created
one hundred poisonous doubles of me.
"They look like real."
They represent
my hundred imagined suicides.

You'll find it difficult, Messenger,
but I know you'll recognize me.
You'll recognize me
by the aura of violet fatigue.
Then we'll sit down at the café
under the umbrellas on the sidewalk.
We will free ourselves of the secrets.
A lot of people will go by
disgusted with history.
They will look at me with sympathy
and whisper to themselves:
Look at that one – talking with himself
without a cell phone.
Then I'll lean on the edge where
everything else begins.
And I'll only feel how love and
freedom merge within me.

THE UNIVERSE IS AN ANONYMOUS CREATOR

For Charles Chu

That Chinese painter we spoke of,
for no reason that we can comprehend,
has turned into a painting by a Chinese painter.
Nothing else about him is known.

We have other names,
a PIN, an ID chip, etc.
Yet, our soul remains impenetrable.

While he—the nameless one—exhibits
only a soul, exposed and lucid.

We contemplate the painting…
While he, through the thin,
peepholes of heaven's doors
carefully and silently examines us.

The Chinese painter, viewed
close-up, is astonishingly modern.
He breaks the visible lines
replacing them with secret links.
He makes signs out of things, and meanings—out of us.

However, viewed from a distance,
the Chinese painter helps
my soul rid itself of time…
And now it makes no difference any more
what dynasty rules over me.

The Chinese painter has taught me
to set the main idea in the corner,
not in the middle of the work.
Because, if we consider the eternal, endless whole,
the empty space is central there.
Nonetheless, the little man—i. e. we,
standing down against the waterfall,
deadens it with our muteness.

Don't sign your work!—
says the little man.—
It's no use.
The Universe is an anonymous creator.

THE BOTTLES

I wake, unlock my eyes
and go out of myself.
The first thing I encounter
are the empty bottles.
Oh, hi, there!
I knew some things
wouldn't abandon me
while I'm wandering about in pink nightmares.
One-eyed, like little cyclopes,
they guard their caves.
And I remember Vanga,
that blind clairvoyant,
who said to Raphael Alberti:
"Poor Spaniard,
all your kin are already dead.
Here they are—
their souls come

and line up like bottles."
Since then I've been taking great care
of the bottles. Because
judging by their circle,
my family of drunks
was quite large.
They claim that the conversation
between the living and the dead
is never listened to.
But, just in case,
I'd better not rattle on
with these empty bottles.
It would be far better to put
an ad in the paper
for all those shipwrecked at the moment:
"Bottles offered—
including the letters
SOS! SOS!—
practically free!"
However,
in this world in which we are awake,
the shipwrecked are far more numerous
than all the ships.
And now no one
throws even a stony glance
at the chasm of the wreckage of others.
Whereas earlier,
with the dignity of the poor,
our mothers exchanged empty bottles
for bread.
Now even this is getting hard,
it seems.
Today, as far as I can see,
even the epoch
is searching for a depot
to deposit our empty words.
And likewise love
returns our empty illusions.
You too, empty heart,
go out and look for
a God who stays open 24/7
so that He might exchange your empty spaces
for a new bottle of the vintage
Universe—made in Bulgaria.

THE LAST CAPRICE

In balance with this life, this death
    —W. B. Yeats

I am walking.
And I am leading my father by the hand.
And he is ever smaller and smaller.
He has lost the key to home.
But he will never admit it.
Like son, like father.
And actually now I don't know
where I could take him.
The Internet-Café
is closed for routine maintenance.
Besides, I don't know
how to open the site
of the Hereafter.
I only know
that the world is a sentence
from a long divine apocrypha.
And I am trying
to build up a home of words.
But it collapses on me.
And I shout:
Oxygen,
help me burn down more quickly!
I feel intolerably wretched!
Iron,
I renounce you!
Damn you, rigidness.
The world is a manner of expression.
Dad,
I don't want to be a father!
I feel terribly wretched.
Mom,
I don't want to become older than you, either!
Allow me this last caprice.
Do something! Please!

You, who are already in the earth,
and the earth has always been in you,
say that you the Goddess-Mother.
And that all things are my brothers.
Allow me to appeal to darkness.
And to sink forever
into her infinite embrace.

PATH

To Georgy Triffonov

Someone is pronouncing you, my friend.
Have you become a prayer by chance?
Someone is checking you like a pulse.
Yet the hand can scarcely feel you.

Stop talking nonsense! You'd better go out jogging.
And you set out. But you look around. And you finally see—
that someone has thrown a dead lamb
onto the path where you used to jog and dream.
The sky is clear. In fact, everything is clear.
The rabid fox barks from the bridge.
Then your soul is overgrown with quietude again.
But the gun's bead has already pinpointed you.

And don't say that these are country scenes.
The sign of the universe is the same everywhere.
Even this stinking twin brother of the Sphinx
reminds you of kings Oedipus and Lear.

The precipice moves its crumbling mouth,
prompting you: Jump down into me! Come on!
No. You will go on along the arrogant path.
No. The local one hundred bagpipes aren't a whiskey brand!

Meanwhile death's skull snarls at the narrow pass.
The crow, the fox, and other characters
pick the carrion clean, change the epochs
and now you don't know whose carcass it is.

Maybe it's that of the little golden lion
that fell from your young hero's little fur cap
when you were in first grade,
leaving you secretly crying.

Today everyone's changing their color or course.
Like guitarists playing all positions.
Are you alone to remain on the merciless path—
strung like a bead on a rosary?

Stop counting prayers and curses.
Once the fox has bitten your footprint,
break the rosary, my friend, and let's disperse

into another, more real, freedom!

This idea, these wild oats
will barely strike a root in my nature.
I take the saddle off the epoch's back
and lie down in the grass to ride, half awake.

Then through dreamy eyelashes I see
how the true path flees from me, leaving me alone
It's so funny and I feel so carefree!
As if I have not yet been born.

THE GARDENS OF ETERNITY

Suddenly
the council of the winds is called.
The clouds remember they're relatives of yours.
And you hear:
"It's high time to take the child
to the zoo."

And you realize that this is a rebuke—a dangerous rebuke
about some quite other, forgotten promise.
And a dark-green morning lies in wait for you
beneath the torture-garden olive trees.

The seventh day has come again.
God is resting.
And you are created.
Entry to the zoo is free today.
The apple glows. The serpent's tongue as well.

The sand along Karl Linne's Alley crunches.
Lazily I am reborn, examine the skies
with amphibian stare.
Is that the place where I will live?
But the family no longer wants me to take them there.

The family tree is rustling malevolently
and all of them are scared.

All of them are bitter.
"Go away!
I don't want to see you, Daddy!"
my future shouts in my face.

He flings the paper bag to the ground.
The ketchup-smothered sandwiches smash
and spread out like the blood of an ancient martyr
whose name has been forgotten.

The branch is broken. Let's not poke about for reasons.
Child, make your own beginning, your own new offshoot,
along which a new eternity can proceed.
And my own end I will invent myself.

But why is no one noticing the split?
People and animals watch each other through the bars.
Meanwhile, I lift the sunset in my hands.
And soon we will vanish without a trace.
I never was as free as now—a beast
having escaped from the political zoo.
So what if across the bridge with its arches of stars
some new century is said to have passed.

I too cross through border forests.
And then I flow into the distant vistas.
Lord, thank you for forgetting
to lock my cage.

A DOUBLE BALLAD

Here it is—the Twenty-first Century—:
a transparent carafe,
into which nothing has yet been poured.
And our voices resound:
"Man is older than the Earth…"

I know what that would mean, were it true.
Okay. Add to the account my years, too.
They are equal to the degrees
of the twice-distilled brandy—
the strong brandy,
which is just about to flow
from the stills to the prophecies
full of lightning flashes.
As for me, I spring from a wilder distillation.
Flowing doesn't cause the fire to grow weaker.
I don't mix with the delicious weakness of weak brandy.

The Twenty-first Century—
a shout of a prophet having fled from a legend.
A waking of a bird.
Or a howl—
rather an echo of a Bacchante in heat
"Evoe!" she cries.
While I keep hearing: "I'm yours!"
(Forgive me, heavenly lips.)

Yet I keep fancying
that my years will suffice
for two lives
of the one and only God.

I peer through the stellar locks to see
who is pretending to be absent there.

And I see myself walking
through ugly cities
with striking girls.

"Take away my reason and toss it up into the sky!"
and I see myself flowing undiluted.
Perhaps a little pungent.
Booze for barbarians,
reaching out for the carafe

of the age, which never came true.
And our voices keep resounding
in your mystic transparence,
Twenty-first Century
of the so-called new epoch,
and second (balladic one) of mine.

RIDGE

> *"Those that I fight, I do not hate.*
> *Those that I guard, I do not love."*
> —W.B. Yeats

I would fall asleep on a summit
and wake up on a coast.
Mystery!
And imagine,
this whore is the mother
of the abandoned plays.
But what is taking place there
behind the curtain
of closed eyes?

There the soul is creeping
along the pale and bare ridge
of what has already been.
A picker of herbs for painkillers,
my soul is moving away,
seeking something lost.
I have lost the ability to get drunk.
Not that I have stopped drinking
illusions.
No. They simply
no longer go to my head.
And how could that not have happened, since
along the pale and bare ridge
war is striding:
warm, cold,
secret, star and global
or God knows what,
striding as slowly as a sower
and scattering the seeds of deadlock.

Nothing sprouts quicker.
And not that bullets don't ripen for me.

Not at all. Simply,
they don't strike me anymore...
And why
all that feverish rushing?
All those Poetry Readings, Spells,
and Salutes to the Fire?
Perhaps if I hadn't glanced
so often at my watch,
it wouldn't be so late.

They wouldn't have erected
that castle of sunset
upon the pale and bare ridge.

What do you think,
old buddy, Peter Curman?
Shouldn't we launch the chariots
around the fortress once again?
The beauties meanwhile madly waving
goodbye to us.
Because I have begun to turn into
a pale and bare ridge
that doesn't know
what elemental reins it holds.
Yet it knows that so far
nothing has kept a curb on me.

THE WALL

We've agreed with the sunset
that we won't look into each other's eyes
while time keeps flowing
and we are part of that same flight.

The woman artist and I have agreed
that she'll go deaf
and I'll go blind.
Thus
maybe at last,
both of us will be doing the same thing.
As in love axioms,
which are not susceptible of proof
but are taken on trust.

This is why I kiss you, approaching sky.
And you, young new horizons,
pale from perspective.

I, too, used to be annoyed
when my mother would draw me close
and kiss me in front of other people,
feeling that she was losing me.

Youth doesn't value such feelings,
unfailing health,
unconquered truth.
Youth prefers
fables and
love.

And look, in rosy haze
the port of the well-invented Ephes
is empty.
The sailors are in the brothel.
Merchants are trying to outwit
each other in the marketplace.
And politicians are squabbling
after the communal midnight feast.
But the swallows are flying lower and lower,
which portends storm,
broken boughs,
falling nests and universes.
From Ephes to the very Alexandria
a-a-a… an apple.
The apple of discord.

Old man, what are you babbling about?
How is it that you have eyes?
Why did Basil II forgive you?
Precisely you?

Look, the mountain
carries skies, it is of use.
Why does it have no eyes,
while you still have them?

I try to argue
that the mountain has lakes.

How original!
Would you like us to turn your eyes into lakes,

from which bitter brooks will flow?
And ask you then:
What do you see? Ah?

I see.
I see the desert,
the global one and promised.
But what are the little children,
the Israeli ones, God's elect, doing there?

We are building up a wall without a temple,
an endless wall is what we're building up,
a new wailing wall.

Eyes, don't say good-bye
to this visible world
and this non-Euclidean space!
For I feel like a manuscript
hidden in the cracks
between the stones of the wall.
Eyes, don't say good-bye!
For I have already been written down
but not yet read.

THE CAT IS DRINKING WATER FROM MY GLASS

For Toma Markov

I know it is a dream.
I know that now
I should move
my hand. Drive it away. And take
a tranquilizer... No,

I can't.

Instead of me,
the reading lamp begins to move..
It takes a different shape,
becomes a starship,
and the little men
get off to take me
as if I were their tranquilizer.

Of course, not the entire me.
My goal,

my axis,
my restless pursuit of an end for itself -
they don't need such things.

They come to wrench from my soul
just one presumptive kernel.
A little ampoule, hidden
behind the wrapping of a glossy consciousness.
But under it…
something mysterious happens.
The little men flee terrified.
But the ship has gone.
I hear a lapping sound… Oh, God!

The cat is drinking from my glass of water.

Thanks, Savior!
Thanks!
Now
my hand will move.
The phantasms will die of fright. And I,
for the lack of a tranquilizer,
will have to gulp down a part of myself…

"You can have some water as well," the cat says.
"For I am only a memory
of your former cat Simmo."
In case you don't believe it,
in case you doubt,
remember Antoine,
remember Lavoisier.

Remember how he was examining water
and instead of a goldfish, he caught
the law, according to which
nothing is created or lost
but only changes its nature…
Then remember the guillotine, where
Lavoisier himself
lost his head.
Adieu, mon cher! Adieu!
Your mother said you shouldn't be afraid.
You won't die in a foreign land.
Beware of water and of fame.
In the present horrid times of kind-betrayers,
against the laws –
create!

NOT FAR FROM THE SHORE

Not far from the shore
I am standing on credible walls.
A useless plant with aerial roots.
And under me seven ages have
already been excavated.
Seven doubles of yours
watch me from under broken helmets.
Troy, Troy, Troy,
how mine you are!
Yet, there is no trace to follow to my own self.
Nothing of what has happened has survived,
except the shadow of the blind poet,
who has hardly been here.
Meanwhile, I'm standing on the walls.
And why should I see
the dirt road and the field,
where rag-countrymen are waving sleeves about?
Whom do they scare?
What do they guard?
Only the bales of straw shine
scattered like plundered sarcophagi.
A fiery wind blows.
and I hear the interrupted phrases of the scarecrow:
Menelaus chased Paris
for the beauty which
didn't save the world.
Achilles fought the duel with Hector
over the corpse of friendship—
the soul's heel.
And you, Time, windy or quiet,
various and continuous,
whom do you fight?!
Is He that strong?
And what's it all about?!
Yet, whatever it's about,
have done with it!
For I am sick and tired
of scaring birds.
I'm already scared myself!

Dauntless little tractors haul
green mountains of watermelons.
Some tourists ask me
whether I am the archeologist.

They blabber that the war is over.
But isn't that red horse grazing
in the bed of a river run dry,
a gift brought by the Greeks?

And the heart is open.

SEMANTIC SEEDS

For Alexander Taylor

Listening to poems in a foreign language—
this indeed seems like
paranormal phenomena,
contacts with nonexistence,
painting a landscape
beyond the mist, ready to tell you:
"Oh, it's not this!
Not this, not this at all!..."

In my neighborhood there is a pipe,
which sings gutter-like
prophecies to the wind.
No clattering of tin. No whistling.
But music.
A melody.
A public prayer.
I have tried to go out in the dead of night to look for it,
to make out the magic.
But it falls silent instantly.
"Don't be afraid!"
I say to it…
I don't care
what follies you spread
but how you do it…

For instance, Lazlo Nod,
Whenever God blessed him with good humor
and illimitable alcohol,
used to translate Bulgarian folk songs.
"Dilmano-Dilbero," et cetera,
meant to him:
"A falcon perched on my shoulder."
Since he was lame,
he had to fly
rather than sow.

A horse had kicked him
in his childhood years
and the older ones were afraid to visit.
Thus he became a big child.
Then—a huge child.
Then—an old child.
I don't remember what language we spoke in
so long with Lazi. Then
the winged horse came to take him back.
Look, yesterday Manuel Muños Hidalgo came.
And the table, redeemed forever,
was filled with Castillian exclamations.
Only the glasses gazed with empty looks
when Manolo said:
"I've come to warn you
that the mold they used for us is broken.
They won't be making the likes of us
anymore."

You must talk with things
in their own fragile tongue. Don't fancy
that they understand yours.
If you find a way, show them
that you test them, the way one tastes
desire or boredom,
or the way one tests a student. Then all
the children will start prompting,
signaling, moving their lips.
And if you grasp one single sign,
you already have a significant captive—
a "Tongue," as they used to say on the front-lines—
a trace of truth resembling
a mark of wing upon the sky,
Begin right now! But don't forget:
only the lie is verisimilar.

So now, having learnt a lesson from my dog,
I bite my leash myself.
This means that I want to go out.
And to think that I am leading my own self myself.
I want to go out of these wicked words,
robbed by politicians,
slobbered over by poets,
stinking of calumny.
I want to go out of them.
And to love you speechlessly.
And to run across that field.
To leap over the magnetic lines.
To follow the scent of the poles
and to contemplate
the ants dragging semantic seeds.
People don't like the singing insects.
People like the fabulous ants.
And they give me the creeps because
the World is a semantic sign
that cannot be pronounced.

A TALE FROM TWENTY-FOUR THOUSAND, FOUR HUNDRED AND FIFTY-ONE NIGHTS

Nevertheless,
some day
I will drink up this damned bottle,
in which
no jinn
has ever been confined
except mine.
But before I leave,
I'll ignite the cork,
just to be sure.

I'll burn it in the ashtray
as if it were a witch.
And with the muddy soot
I'll paint
a black (but not pessimistic)
eye on my forehead
or rather between my forehead and the wall,
which no one could break down.
Yet so many others have collapsed!

"I am the one-eyed one!"
the smoke will utter, rising,
abandoning the fire
(just as my truest little comrades
abandoned me).

I wonder, is there anyone left to say:
"Blinded dreams,
I will lead you
and I will even tell you what can be seen
on both sides of the road.
What is seen,
what is seen…is space.
Yet no time
can be seen."

We keep stumbling along the road sought
by the Phoenician King Agenor's
kidnapped daughter.
Which way are his
signs,
signs,
signs
pointing…
But that happened earlier.
And now it's later.

On the celestial display
quietly rise
star wars.

The swindler has gone before us.
And has left
the doors of words open.
The wind is blowing!
It keeps invoking memories.

And the warmth of sentiment grows cold.
And the pipes
along which thought runs
are cracking.
And the glittering ice
strikes roots into dark nothingness.
And is that writing?
Is that speech?
Or are these signs?—
Stolen, crumpled, torn-up, greasy signs
through which the bottom of the bottle
already appears.

This is how the world has gone out of itself.
And in the empty smoky space
the waitress is seated
on the adjacent era.
She has taken off one of her shoes,
wriggling swollen little toes.
And she is writing down
a short story of digits.
"Hey, girl,"
I say,
because I feel like saying something to someone,
"would you tell me a story?"
She gasps:
"Are you nuts, old man?"
which means: Request denied!
"Come on, what's the matter?!
I just want you to narrate my conscience to sleep,
lest I should look at
what's happening around me."
"I know what you're looking at.
But watch out I don't call the barman
to tell you the ending
before you know the beginning."
"If that's what you think,
lie low, Scheherazade's asshole!
I can narrate my sleeping pill
myself."
Once upon a time,
(somewhere between the twentieth
and the twenty-first moments
after the end of history),
there was, you know, one more pitiful ending—
the creature Visionary vanished

from the dying human species.
It became extinct because
it ceased believing
in miracles.
So then dreams went blind.
Because they see
only with visionary's eyes,
having none themselves.

And then
the age of blind luck reigned:
some ate and drank.
while all the rest had little fun.
Finally,
before closing, a madman
suddenly got up and painted that eye on himself…
And people started dreaming again…

The barman dreamily calls the waitress
into the small backroom behind the bar.
She walks past me,
shakes the bottle
and exclaims:
"It's as empty as your head.
Now shake a leg,
because we're gonna sweep away reality."

ULTIMA VERBA

Sometimes it seems to me
that once
everything was a beginning
or in the beginning,
or before that.
And I used to cast myself forward to finish,
                                        to finish.
The way you put out a fire,
lest you go up in flame.
The way you plug up a hole,
lest you sink.
The way you love for the first time
not caring why
or in order to end carelessness.

But, you see, of late,
something draws me to begin,
                              to begin.
And perhaps it's indeed the ultimate time.
I begin a new building on top of the ruins.
I build a wall, and dig, and fill,
until I hear:
"My God!
But you... what are you doing?
You said that you were planting a bush,
yet passion sprouts,
yet fury sprouts!.."
And I watch the crazy plant
with sin-bearing blossoms
and fruit
of the forbidden knowledge.
It is a plant I know.
And I'm ashamed, I'm ashamed
of the present historical tense,
of the shameless tense
with verbs stripped bare.
"I swear to you!
This is impossible!
I planted two little seeds!
I planted Ultima Verba!"
Night passes beneath my window
talking to someone:
"A willow tree?!"
That's a wretched substitute
for the Judaic palm tree, for the olive tree..."
But we feed
not on
only what is spoken,
but only
on what has been understood.

And sometimes it seems to me
that this world is made
of the ultimate words
of other worlds.
Quite other. Quite vanished...
And then I feel
I'm one of them.

THE STONE

Almost like Sisyphus
and quite like myself,
I heave the stone a little.
Round as a cloud.
Dark as thunder.
Yet what a silence reigns!
Beneath the stone sleeping Evil lies,
a coiled centipede—
a black galaxy with head laid
on a pillow of a martenitsa…
If someone's watching me,
he must be puzzled.
I have to figure out
something comprehensible,
so that the dwarf pats me on the shoulder,
"Good!
You are one of us again…"

I heave the stone
to hide time under it—
the time I stole.
"Why, where can one
steal time?"
Of course I answer you:
From one's self.
Only from one's self.
Most easily, from one's own sleep.
And hardest of all—from one's own work.
"And why steal?…
And from yourself at that…
And time at that!"
To give Love
something purely mine.
"And she? What did she say?"
She told me that she couldn't possibly accept
a gift so dear.
She wouldn't like to feel
obliged… To be bound…
That sort of thing.

I used to fix the price of time
according to the pain of parting.
"Time is money"—
to me that was merely

a proverb,
spread by
proverbial Franklin.
However, when I found out
that everyone thinks so,
when I saw
my present—a withered
posy, left
without water,
I made up my mind to bring
time back, where
it had been—in me. Then
the stolen time smiled at me:
"Everything comes back, my boy:
the departed swallow,
the prodigal son,
the stolen horse,
the lost hope...
Everything comes back, my boy,
only time,
only time
never returns!
And look
the cunning metal device
walks across the desert Mars.
It's seeking water.
I am hardly so thirsty.
But I too
am seeking something.
I'm looking for a proper place.
And I look with one of my eyes
at what that one, the metal one is doing.
Everything there is stone.
Why doesn't it think
of lifting up one too?
And what will happen
if a martenitsa flares up again
under it.
You wonder what?
I'll tell myself:
This is a proper place
to close my eyes.

ASHES OF LIGHT

    I

I have found a house,
older than the universe.
And master-builders turned up right away.
Well, you've bought,
quite a white elephant there,
they said.
Actually, old age is irremediable.
Better to pull it down
and make
something entirely new
out of the material,
as the last of the leaders used to say.
But you don't seem convinced,
so make your repairs.

I said: "I'll think about it."

    II

All night long my lantern burns.
I can think in the dark just as well.
But I take delight in seeing
how the sunset nestles into me,
and how in the morning
it tiptoes away.
And I pretend that I don't hear.

    III

The room looks like a lantern
and I,
perhaps,
like a wick burning low.
Ashes of light.
Nocturnal creatures bat against
my glass walls.
Enormous moths with crimson eyes
on their wings keep fluttering about.
You are like us, they say to me,
only you have wings on your eyes.

    IV

And in the morning, the birds wake me up.
Their little beaks are knocking,
announcing a tranquil destiny.
In fact, they breakfast on the moths
stuck on the window-panes.
Then they tell me:
Beware of the master-builders!
They are keen on making repairs
because there is a legend:
in the foundations of this house
is hidden the treasure
of the dead caravan.

    V

What demon has started the rumor
that in the foundations of this world
there is a treasure
of virgin happiness?

I don't mean sphinxes
sacred chalices,
talking tablets
and alchemic witchcraft…
Yet, the caravan of time
is loaded with secrets,
isn't it?

    VI

Since I am too shy to beg,
I adjure:
Be wary of
the master-builders
who offer
to repair our world.

DISTANCE XXI

"You're so far away,"
you whisper in my ear.
Instead of kidding around,
you'd better fasten your seatbelt!
I am fastened to those same circumstances.
The stewardess, expressionless as a ghost,
demonstrates how to put on
and inflate a life jacket.
All too frequently now
display replaces hope.
Everything is always explained
in two languages.
One of them is as condemned as love.
I think God spoke in fewer words.
Take a look at which are His
and which have been made up
later on
by us.
And choose for the two of us
something unique,
something condemned…
No,
distance isn't
such an almighty cause.
As is the case with flying,
it's more important how many wings you'll change,
at how many airports you'll be waiting
for the fog to lift…
I hate this impenetrable emptiness.
So, first kiss me.
Then I'll confess to you:
We can't fly for long.
We land too often.
We have to check
whether the Earth has fled.
We have to drink the melting snow—
it is Eternity in a state of change…
Now we are rising
over the dark predictions.
Our phones are turned off,
lest we be troubled
by the cries for help,
by the gurgling of cut throats
or by the gunshots within the temple…

It's time for emergency measures!
It's time to take prints
from fate's finger.
The world situation is dualistic.
But when was it not?
The Virgin has given birth to twins.
Apropos,
I saw such a painting
at the cheerful exhibition
"Rubens' Years" or something like that.
The author hadn't had the courage to sign his name.
They had removed the haloes of infants.
To humiliate them completely,
they had placed them
on welfare...
Only an eagle is entitled to two haloes.
All of us are looking suspiciously at one another.
One of us is a terrorist.
One of us will blow up the flying heart.
Or will be shot before that
by the friendly fire
of liberty.
And this will happen within us,
not somewhere else.
So, darling,
I'm not that far
from the truth.

IRISH FANTASIES

To Celia and Jack

1.

The ninth wave has cast me up
upon the isle of Ackel.
Around me the rocks are smoldering
like bits of cinder
fallen from the northern lights.
Magic streams
flow down from the nothingness
and merge together.
And the waterfalls of Dookinella
bark now and then like dogs
made up by Heinrich Böll.

Of course, I think about
the parting. And "I drink
to keep my soul and body
separate,"
as Oscar Wilde said.

Otherwise,
everything is
simple and lonely.
And the clouds keep quiet.
As if
God is writing His memoirs.

A repentant devil whets His lightning
and I slowly turn into an island.
According to the bell that is impossible
but in Connemara they sing a song,
according to which
along the road northwestwards
slow things happen.

    2.

The strangely humble cottage
of the Nobel laureate,
after his death was turned into
a home for strangers,
for poor wretches writing memoirs
and drinking "Paddy."
All night long the rain returns
to knock at the windows
like a drunkard.

I conceal the fact that I feel cold.
But Jack Harte, the Ambassador of birds,
goes out and returns with a pail of peat.
The fireplace bursts into flames
with the smell of malt.

They say claustrophobia
is a disease of poets.
It catches me
when I think about the German
locked up in himself.
Then I start to feel pressed for room
within myself.
The adjacent fence is made of barbed wire

that in its turn is wrapped in thick undergrowth
with crimson blossoms
called Christ's tears...
Yet, in spite of that,
or maybe just because of that,
everything has managed to escape,
everything that
had any meaning.

Now I feel so bookish,
that I am writing on my own self—
unrepentant and
with unsharpened lightning flashes.

   3.

I return to Dublin
like a bolt out of the blue.
What, damn it, have you been doing up there?!

Dublin's chimneys
are arranged
like mouth organs,
like Latin libraries
or Russian Katyushas.
Or maybe they are combs
for combing rain clouds.
But they don't suspect it
and they imagine
that they are mystic crowns.
"Lord!" they say, "What a small world,
and what a large number of rulers we got to be!"

And it seems they are right.

If a star falls down,
it serves it right.
If a ruler falls down,
what a laughter will follow.
But if a chimney falls!—
It is an omen
for the entire universe,
which is already choked with smoke.
And everyone rushes forward
to lift the chimney up again—
the fire's crown,
the raven's rostrum.

And let God lift His nose
from the blurred screen.
Let Him turn off the computer
and conclude:
There is a time for everything.
A time for memories.
And a time to wear a nightcap.
And a murmur follows:

Goodnight, light.
Bye-bye, God!

LULLABY

The boy was standing at the exit
of the new gas station
like a deadlock,
like a gas pump,
like an air hose.
I braked suddenly to pick him up.
And only then did I notice
what an evil appearance he had.
I asked him:
"Which way?"
"To Plovdiv," the hitch-hiker grumbled.
"Eh!" I joked bluntly like an intellectual.
"Such a young boy
to such an old city!"
"Oh, fuck this face of mine!
Could you, too, guess
that I still have no ID card?"
"But why are you cursing?"
"Because they won't give me a job.
I can't get started.
Do you know what it's like
to be
and yet be unable to make a start?…"
I gave him a piece of chocolate.
He ate it up at once

and fell asleep.
I watched him, just in case,
in the rearview mirror,
rocking
in the loop of sleep.
His hair, long as a wig,
made him look like
a premature Robespierre.

And so we flew across eternity
like two centuries,
like two tenses:
past continuous
and a future that cannot begin.
Meanwhile the whirling wind hummed a lullaby:
Sleep, sleep, my boy.
It's not your face that's to blame,
but our shameless falseness.
Sleep, but don't trust Fukuyama.
History exists.
History is searching.
And soon
it will find you a job.
Oh, what a job!
They will remember you!

SMS

For Iva

Did you see the sign of the sunset?
A field sown with secrets.
Rays sprout among the clouds.
Late birds
gracefully alight
and peck early-risen stars.
I only know that these are not landscapes.
Everything is silent and impossible.
Ask the sky what it wants to say..
You can.

INSOMNIA

Quite close by,
behind the corner of the world,
shines the nonstop
Internet Café.
What was there earlier?
Well, I don't remember.
We gave technology for that
Electronic databanks of the universal knowledge.

Sometimes my dog
takes me out for a walk
after midnight.
The air is dirty.
The trees are drugged.
Life – imaginary.
His snout touching the blue shopwindow,
my best friend watches
the café's mystic interior.
At this hour it is
empty and interstellar.
The computers look like
urns for dead time.
Just one display is glimmering.
The hacker is sitting in front of it.
He is creating a virus.
He is sipping cold coffee and dreams
of deleting the memory of the Universe.
What will the world soul do then?
Where will it hide?
What will it pretend to be?
"It serves it right," the hacker says.
And the dog is bewildered.
He starts shivering like a
clairvoyant in a trance.
Perhaps he sees how the virus
is devouring the past
and over chaos hovers
just a lonely, endless
and uncertain global future.

NIGHT KNIFE

Ibid.
There is no change.
No stars. The only street
lights are a few shopwindows
and a sign.
Further down is the disco.
Taxicabs—yellow dogs—squatting
in front of the butcher's
for tender flesh.
But nowadays no one abstracts such concepts.
Whereas here it's different. Here
there is a living soul.
It belongs to the guard, who keeps an eye on
the chairs and tables
in front of the new pub.
He has leaned his back on the blackboard
with the unwiped menu.
He has wrapped himself up
like a sensitive, shivering scarecrow.
Nothing can be seen of the soul,
but it sees everything.
The scarecrow sees how
the infinitive tense appears,
how the shade of Time sways.
And halts
abruptly…
"That's the thief!"
the guard whispers.
"That's the criminal element.
But what's it doing there? Did it fall asleep?
If so
day will never break!"
And the night guard moves in Time's direction,
armed with just a night knife—
a pocket one, but sufficient.
On his soul's back—
a chalky price.
Whereas everything else is priceless.
And while we ask ourselves:
"Is that life?"
Time is suddenly gone,
leaving only
a yellow puddle.
And on the wall, among the meaningless graffiti,
a few more scribbles:
God forgives.
TIME —doesn't!

SPIDERMAN

In the garden,
in front of the windmill,
not on the bench
but on the grass,
the Spiderman is sitting.
He's opened his paper,
pretending to read the spider's web,
while listening to
the desperately buzzing
captured news.
But no one pays any attention
to that postmodern piece of plastic art,
except the birds, who are curious
if the flies are real
or fake.
Of course, they are fake—
ready to become history.

Oh, sparrows! Oh, shaggy guttersnipes,
oh, who don't even make nests.
Otherwise, I would have assumed
that it was you, who made us.
Because,
man abandoned by history
is like an abandoned nest.

The inhabited nest
knows it's worthwhile.
Songs come floating out of it.
And that's worthy of praise.

The abandoned nest broods ghosts.
There is a time for making nests,
the Preacher will say.
Then God provides
his special mud.
Nature provides the straw.
We—labor.
And here comes history.
And lays its cuckoo's eggs
in us.
Some kick them out of the nest at once.
Others listen carefully:
What is it moving about in there?
"Gosh, it's my heart,"

the others say.
And a new minor history
with a cannibal's little beak
hatches from the heart.

Man, possessed of history,
wants to fly away from himself.
He flaps the wings
he doesn't have.
He is great, if he perishes.
He is wretched, if he survives.
For it's not him but history that flies off.
Then he climbs down
his thin
posthistoric thread
into the nothingness.
Into ordinary time,
which has neither cause
nor consequence.
There, in the garden
of the windmill
(which is grinding unity
into powder),
the Spiderman,
thin-legged
and big-bellied,
is knitting his newspaper, thinking:
If a strong wind blows,
it will bring down the old nests.
That's fine.
But it will also turn over this page.
And then something new may happen.

FALL

Mornings I wander upwards to the forest waterfalls—
tiny children's toys lost by the gods.
Older than the forest, younger than the heavens,
I still feel like playing. I can still be taken by surprise,

being various, yet the same, whereas they are always different.
I called one "My" so it wouldn't be without a name.
It is sunny there. I strip down to my waist.
But I visit it in the winter too…

So even in the bitter cold, I set forth again. And through the mist,
there on the cliff, I saw, instead of the waterfall, a fallen angel,
a quiet, icy body with stooping wings
and a fox licking its tears before running away.

The boreas had toppled down two spruces
as if it wished to carry the wounded creature
on a stretcher from a Simberg painting.
Meanwhile, I keep on asking myself absurd questions:

Why do white angels visit us more and more seldom?
Why is the soul's luminous ecstasy breaking apart?

Why does every faith begin in love and end in cruelty
with broken wings of victories, angels, and ideals?
But the next day there was just a tiny cloud sailing way up high.
The waterfall boomed—a white wind had blown past from Drama or Kavala.

GALLERY III

ARTWORK BY

STOIMEN STOILOV

Green-Wnged Horse

Gallery III

Green-Wnged Horse

Gallery III

Green-Wnged Horse

Gallery III

Green-Wnged Horse

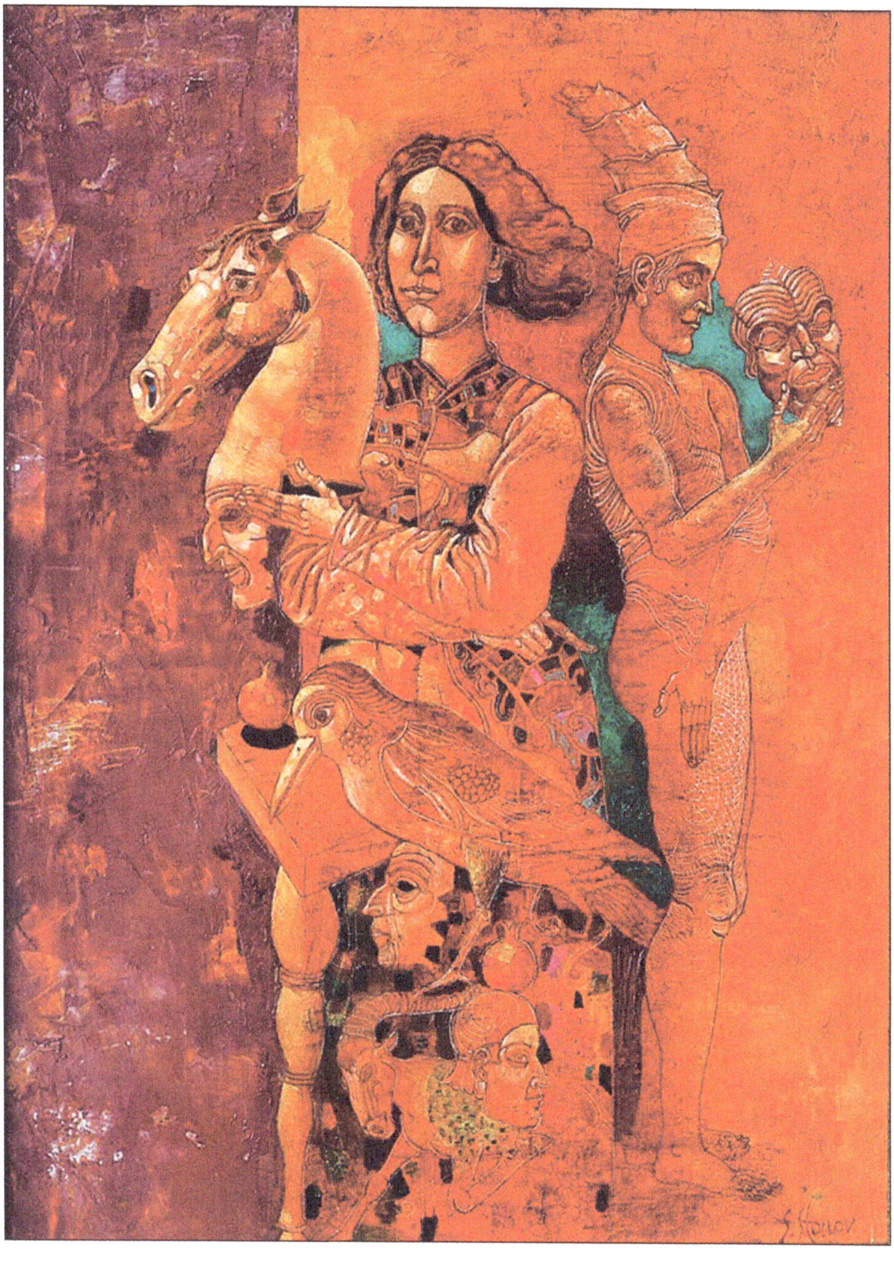

Green-Wnged Horse

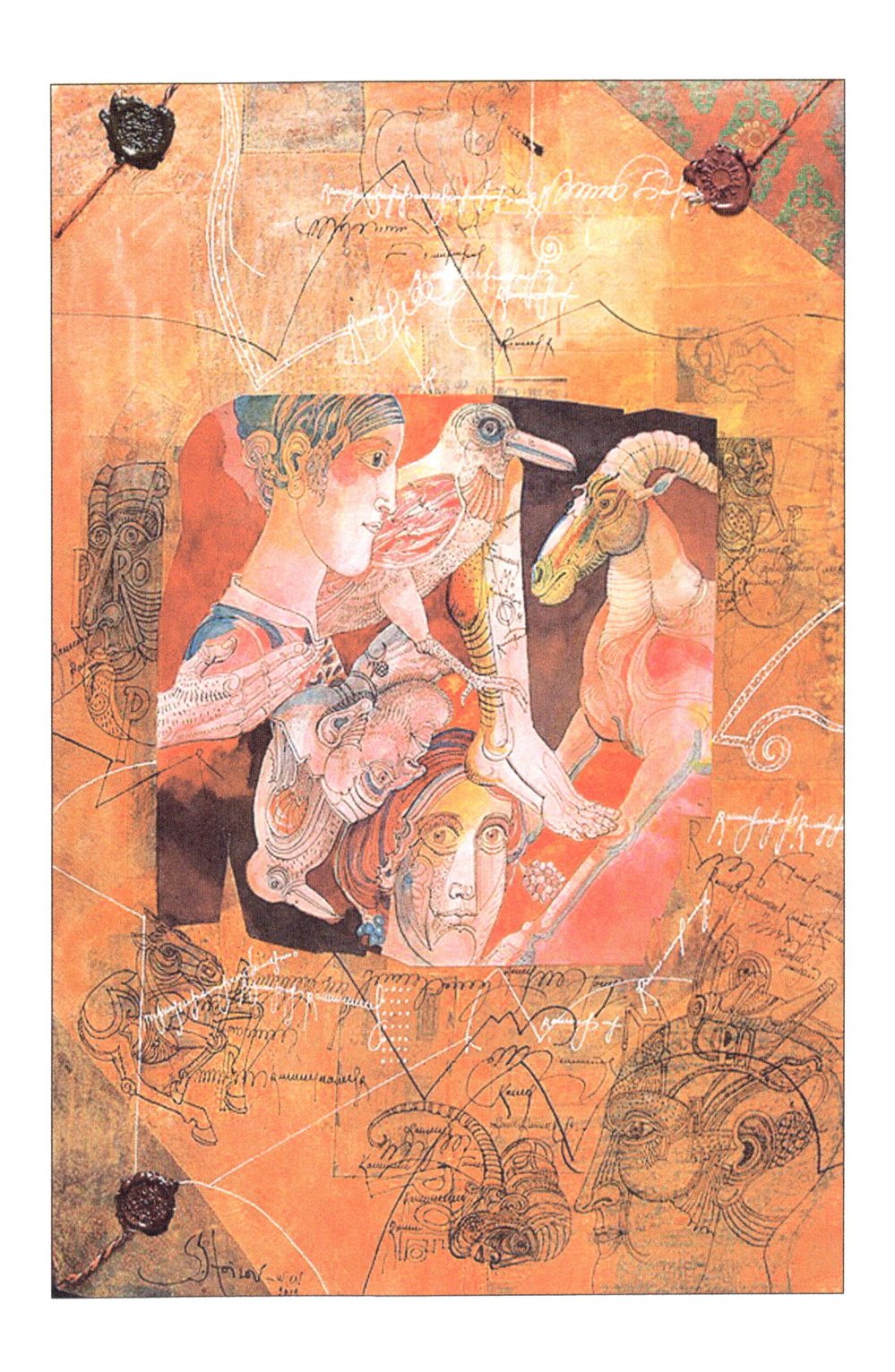

Gallery III

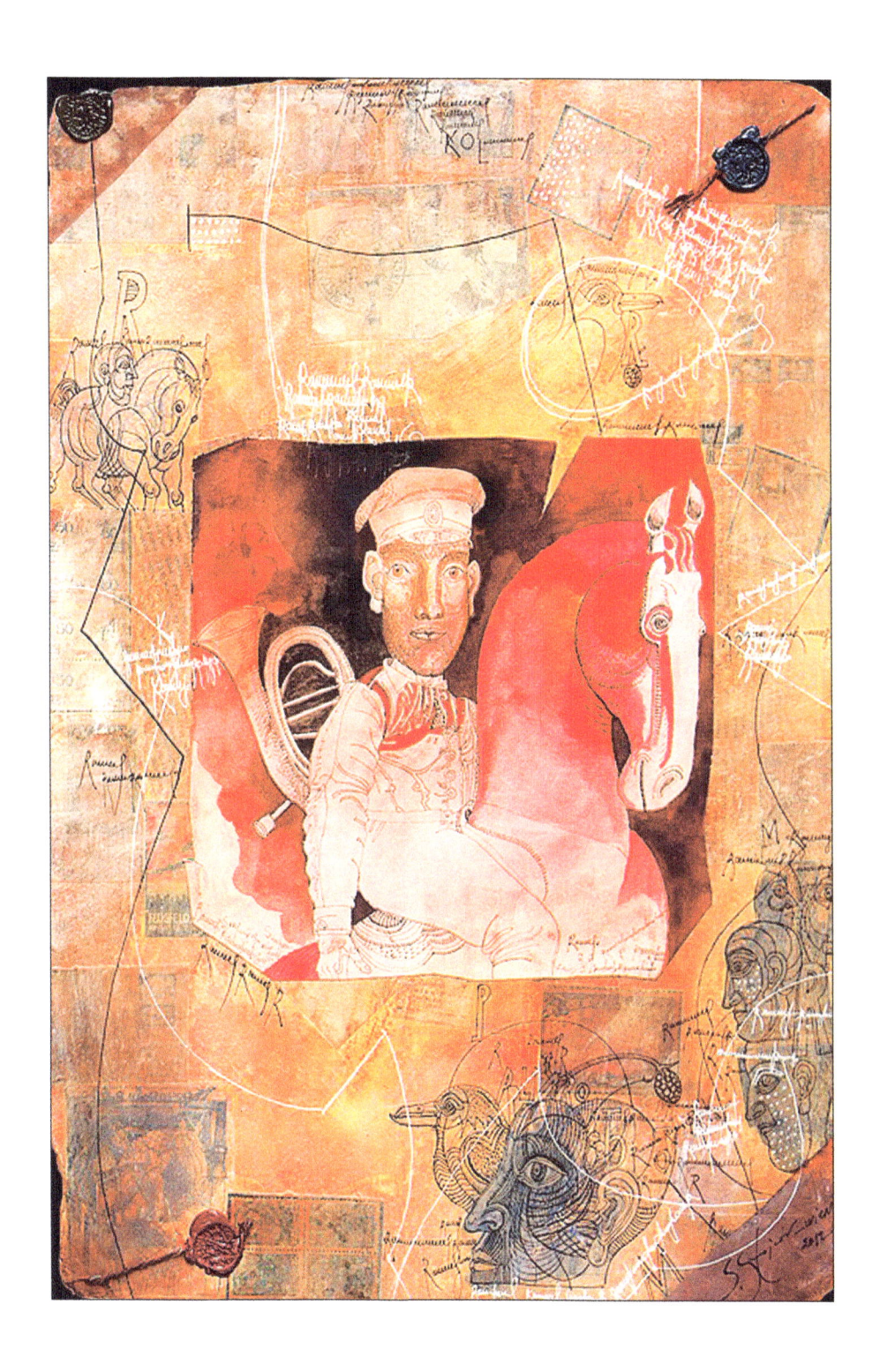

Green-Wnged Horse

Gallery III

OTHER PREVIOUSLY PUBLISHED POEMS

A SONG TO GARCIA LORCA

> *"When I die...*
> *bury me with a guitar..."*
> —Garcia Lorca

Where is that gory Granada?
Where is your grave?
Whom should I ask?
The fiery horses that snort
and scrape the earth with
restless hoofs, or the bearded
eagles of rugged Nevada?...

Granada is too far away...
Are the skies there blue or gray?
Are the myrtles green?
I don't know.
But I do know that you died for Granada,
that the blood-stained shirts
of brothers of mine have rotted
in the Spanish earth, where
the seguidilla's heard ...

Granada is far away, but you are not.
I want to find your grave not to cry
and grieve, but to sing a song and
pick the waiting strings of my guitar
I want to whet on the stone of your grave
a Castilian knife of the strongest metal
for the coming battle.

A SONG ABOUT LIGHTNING RODS

How often you go unnoticed.
How often we don't even realize
you are there. The sun alone,
at sunset, gilds your swords.
It's absurd to compare
this enigmatic flame
with flashing neon signs,
with the fashionable
tube-like torches,
or with the benches on which
neighborhood women sit
commenting on endless yesterdays,
or with the fountains where
young flirts meet new boyfriends.

But when the sky frowns down,
and the earth is struck dumb,
and the furious storm
rips off posters from the walls,
the benches become ludicrous,
and the neon sign shivers shamefully.

Only you in an electric terror,
and above everything, stand confidently.
A thunderbolt hurtles over the platinum.
Afterwards, a sunny calm will spread out
far and wide and you will disappear
amid the chimneys, proud and
inconspicuous once again.

APPASSIONATO

I love the night sky
for it alone is naked.
Daylight prevents me from
watching the universe's nakedness.

Ah, that starry nakedness!

Don't dress! I want to watch you,
to unravel your substance
which attracts me so imperiously.

Love me!
Be my night!

TANGO

There is another earthly sphere
where everything is void of meaning.
Everything
except –
that you've come
that you're with me…
And that you're drinking a small chocolate brandy.

And the bad weather will be wonderful!

The rain will begin its career
as a pointillist, so that you'll stay
a long time, long time…

You are the one who makes things beautiful.
Even the broken umbrella stand.
Even the run in your stocking,
fixed with nail polish.

And also, you don't realize
how beautiful you are….

There is another earthly sphere.
Why are you so jealous of me,
begrudging me the wind
and the evening's fading light
on the mountains?

POSITIONS

We are not schoolmates;
nor have we struck a friendship
over a glass of brandy.
We have taken positions
in the same trench where
two worlds are warring.

The world of the gods at twilight
counter-attacks every day.
The hours flow quickly like blood.
It is so good you are next to me!
I thank you without a word, a look.
We don't even know each other's names.
That is why as bullets whistle by
we are brothers.

But when this battle ends,
we shall search each other's eyes, and
probably we shall be amazed to find,
that they are absolutely different.
You'll say, "I am fond of silence."
I'll say, "I am fond of jazz."
We'll smile at our names.
And then: "Good-bye!"
It won't be late, nor early,
for the unknown winds,
and unknown birds.
Only those who die will
keep their positions.

MY MOTHER IN PARADISE

The little angels you stitch,
with what is left of your
blue eyes, the good little angels
such as I myself once was
at their age, the little angels,
mother, the little angels
are waiting for you to stitch
the last tiny wing.

Then they will begin to sing
and will flutter around you.
They will turn loose your hair –

thin and white. And you'll ascend
with them as the saints did.

There, in Paradise,
will commence your sufferings.
Because in Paradise there is nothing
that looks like your son.

You will fall down before the Almighty's
throne. You'll wash his feet with your tears.
And you will pray to him,
you'll pray to let you go back home,
unseen, just for a minute.
To prepare something for my breakfast.
To brush my clothes...
And to write down
on my cigarette pack: "Come back early!"

The Almighty will smile.
Although he is also embroidered
with the blue of your eyes.

And he won't grant your wish.

You will recline alone
beneath the blissful palms.
And with a hairpin you'll pierce
in the sky a starlet, a secret brilliant
star, to watch our neighborhood.

The windows of the white apartment
buildings will light up. In the shadows
couples in love will stand like statues.
Women in slippers will go for bread
and will call out to their children
in a sing-song voice.
A Caravelle will hover above the airport.
Invisible trains will whistle through the night.

Ah, the whistles of those night trains,
by which I'm always somewhere traveling.

You've heard them. Listen, listen to them.
Hear how they come, hear how they rush,
how they roar at the railroad crossing.
One of them will be my hoarse and
belated cry for you, mother.

DAYTIME MOON

The world is made of
earth, sky and questions.
I too, like everyone,
am trying make things clear,
to turn form into formula,
and knowledge into usefulness...
But why, when reading the latest
news in the tram, or later on,
when listening to my boss's
pompous voice, why do I keep
an eye on the sky? Why?
Daytime moon, do I feel your
presence, barely noticeable,
like the scar of a vaccination?
Why also, in the cafeteria
or when finishing an urgent article,
I keep thinking of you?
You distract me, daytime moon,
a transparent white ghost, a secret.
Why are you there on such
a sunny afternoon? Have you
stayed behind, or are you premature?
This might be all the same to you…
But not to me! I am transient.
Short-lived like my verse.
I am looking for the clarity of things...
Oh, bridal veil, torn apart
and thrown into the blue!
Are you last night's memory
or a presentiment of the future?...

SOUL

This morning I woke up
so suddenly
that my soul
had no time to turn into an abstraction.

It was just
so amusing to watch
how it leapt outdoors,
arid, transforming itself
into sky and branches...

I've always known I'm being spied upon.
But this sky!
And these branches!
They're so familiar to me!

Sunrise.
Breeze.
Soot from the Hydro-Electric Plant…
I've always called them –
my eastern window.

Actually, I don't like these branches.
Last years' leaves
don't want to fall off.
The new ones
proliferate without restraint.
And the end result is something tasteless.
Something like two tickets
for the same seat.
And quarrels with usherettes.
But the only thing is that I have no right
to grin
once it is
my own soul.

Really…
Why can't I
Forget anything of late?
Why can't I lose anything?!
Tear something to pieces!
And throw it away!…

If I hear a noise
as if
a child has showed its hand in the candy box –
that means
that the old leaves are rustling.

If the sound is quiet
and reminds me
of the undressing of a girl –
that means that the new leaves are rustling…

—But you don't love me anymore! –
she tells me.
And I said nothing…

Wretched, flighty soul!

POEM

    1.

To be able to reach you,
my dearest friends,
I cover immense distances.

    2.

The one
who has baptized
the mountains and the rivers,
the chasms and objects,
has not been able to come up
with names for my roads.

    3.

That is why I find it difficult to tell you everything.
(Words are too crude a wrapper
for what I want to confide in you.)

    4.

That is why I keep mum sometimes.

    5.

My blood is of the "O" Group—
to everyone I can give,
but from everyone I cannot take.

    6.

That is why I keep mum.

    7.

I make haste to rejoice
over the quietly
shed smile.

    8.

At your complicity in the azure of the sky.

CARMEN

or the Imaginary Girl

Some time ago,
some pearly time ago,
before the holidays,
in the phantom some time ago—
we used to turn into green giants.
We used to drink beer with cognac.
We used to smoke long cigarettes with golden tips.
We used to tell each other our amorous escapades...

Precisely then I imagined
    the imaginary girl.
It was my turn, and I still
had nothing to reveal.
And then I imagined that we had kissed
behind the electric-transformer station.
And that we have our own tune—
"Tell me, Carmen, love me, dost thou... ?"

They all laughed at me, of course.

But during the night, when all alone
and very young, I was composing dark verses,
someone whistled up to my window beckoning:
"Tell me, Carmen, love me, dost thou... ?"
I opened it, trembling like a flame,
and spied you, so desirable,
my beauty, with hair, blown by
by the midnight wind and lit by the moon,
and with a whisper like iris petals:
"Here I am! As you imagined me!
Call me Carmen! And know that I love you..."

Oh, my dear Carmen! How many times
you have come to embrace me, caressingly,
either to excite me on to victory
or to sooth me in my suffering.

Axioms repeatedly betrayed me.
Brothers in arms betrayed me.
And I alone betrayed myself...
And only you, the imagined one,
to this very day have never betrayed me.

When the road wandered far from me,
you remained with me.
When the bullets were finished
you remained with me.
And you did not ask anything else
except one boyish whistling.
"Tell me, Carmen, love me, dost thou...?"

Be with me again tonight, beloved!
Kiss my hair, which is already turning white.
Keep kissing me. Drink away my fire!
For I feel I am burning to ashes.
And the wind dissipates me in time.
And I understand – and all some day
will understand – that in reality
the imagined one was I.

AFTER FINISHING THE COGNAC

Now go away all of you,
you well-wishers and advisers,
concerned about what I should be.
I want to be the tin cap on a lemonade bottle.
I want my daughter, while dressing
in the morning, to hide me
in the tiny pocket of her apron
so that she has something private
at the kindergarten.
For it is not allowed
to bring in such things there.
Yet they are so necessary.

When needed, I'll suddenly
begin to glow, serrated,
silver, star-like. And
my daughter will smile…

So, let the ban be broken!

THE GOOD SAMARITAN

I walk along an ancient country road,
cut by Caterpillar chains.
Forgotten green. In the cathedral
of the empty afternoon silence
gives me the sacrament and I become
good, almost as good
as the good Samaritan.
I walk along an ancient country road,
admiring the sunflowers, admiring
their loyalty, how all of them, but all
and really all are looking at the sun!
And how they look at it!...
But see, there is among them
one, a single one, that has
turned its back to the sun.
It immediately becomes my sunflower.

I run towards it. Prickly leaves
lick my cheeks. I stumble over
lumps of earth and stubble.
I embrace my sunflower
and lovingly try to show it
what the right direction is.

Without a word it turns again
towards the heretical side.
The sunflower is mad.
It is fanatic. Having stared
at the sun too long, it looks like
the sun. I try to discover
what it is staring at.
There is just the sky
and nothing else.
Dark blue ridges,
the smoke of a train,
a slow, distant, ghost...

My confused friend,
tell me something about
your imaginary sun!
Is it square? Is it black?
Is it some obscure creature?
A lonely testament?
A soldier's wound?...

My sunflower keeps
a scornful silence.
Brown ants creep up
along the stems of all
sunflowers and mine as well.
The stream of a jet plane
curves overhead like a whip.
I walk along an ancient country road.

GUNSHOT

They left me in a tree,
on a small balcony among
the boughs, called a stand…
Then the sleigh glided away.
The little bells of childhood
died away. I was left alone.

I was left alone in the last
forest of my world.
A forest with beasts
and forest spirits, and
silence, resinous and cold.

I felt that I was freezing
in the silence.
I pulled back the breech and
stared through the barrel.
And through it I saw
the volcano Fudjiyama –
the placid sacred mountain…
Or perhaps I saw death
lying in wait. And since
I know that death does
not wait long, it has no time,
I quickly plugged up my end
with two good cartridges for deer.

Then I heard the deer drawing near.
His horns were crackling through
the bush like a rising fire.
At the end of the clearing
he looked around. And he bowed.
I'd say he wished to kiss the earth.
But in fact, he was looking for the salt.

I took aim, held my breath.
And the scarlet whip cracked
with frightful strength.

The deer jumped straight
towards the sky like a fountain
with whose tap children play.
And then it broke down in the snow.
Then the mysterious skirmish started.
Agony, resembling amatory madness.
Love with the nothingness. O, death!

I climbed down from the stand.
With the second bullet I shot
him in the head to keep from
spoiling the deerskin. I took out
the fuming fired cartridges, but
dropped them in the blood
because right then above me
flew the deer's soul.
Did the forest groan?
The last forest of my world.
And the exhausted wind.

POSE 13

With immense delight
they come to pose.
In the dirty studio they freeze,
as if for eternity itself.

But, it is precisely this
eternity destroys them.

After fifteen minutes
they grow nervous, ask for a cigarette.
And they groan as if
they have already endured
fifteen centuries. Then
to all of them it suddenly
occurs that they have some
important appointment, or
business meeting, or concert.

And they're on their way!

My wife is an artist.
She knows that this will
happen with each of them
very soon. She rushes during
those fifteen minutes to grasp
the eternal from the person—
The proud eyes. The intelligent
forehead, the casual, radiant smile.
Or even modesty – yes, modesty itself!
Because the person grows tired
and his pose turns prosaic.

And they're all on their way!

Then I enter the studio.
Then my hour strikes!
My wife sits me down in the place
vacated by the person who has already left.
She anesthetizes me with two or three kisses,
perfumed with turpentine. And continues.

And thus I pose all day long for many a day
for someone else's leg, for someone else's arm,
for a shoulder, for a chest, or for everything else…
Sullied with someone else's splendor.
Inspired like a child playing a game:
Tsar, to you, Happy Name Day.
And I must tell you that I persevere.
I just sit there and think about
all kinds of things. I just sit there
and think to myself. Sometimes I
imagine how fame walks with my feet.
How it scratches itself with my hand.
And when I have a foretaste how I will haunt –
a faceless and nameless nonentity –
through the halls of eternity, inside me
it becomes terribly beautiful and funny.

"Hey!" My wife's getting angry behind the easel.
"Didn't I tell you that you're supposed to look dreamy!
What are you grinning at, like an idiot?"

So I nail myself back into the pose again.
"Sorry," I say, "but I started thinking about something.

COCKFIGHT

"Club de Playa Pachacamac"

An amphitheater and an arena for
two thousand folks or for a universe…
Not that it matters any more.
For they are bringing in the gamecocks,
dressed in velvet cloaks. They fasten
razor blades to their legs and
present them then to the umpire.
And the entire crowd of emperors
is choosing now its gladiators...
"Bets? Place your bets!
Place your bets, señores!"
Meanwhile, they are playing Bolero
up there.
"One hundred sols on the right one!"
"One hundred sols on the left one!"
"One million on the ultra-left one!"
"One million on the ultra-right one!"

Within seconds the cocks will be a ball
of blood and one of them will be the winner.
He'll later die, behind the scenes,
while the bank counts its proceeds.

It's just the same in life, goddammit.

The bets are somewhat higher.
But the end, the end is so alike.
Death for the clowns of politics!
Death for the word-mongers!
Death for the muggers! Though
they are often honest little people...

I too have been to funny battles.
I have killed. And I have been killed.
And I have been blinded by the bloody shine.
And my beak has been filled with sand.

While up there, in the amphitheater,
those unbelievable Peruvian women
with their eucalyptus figures
have been dissolving in the wind…

So that is why, I'm not at all indifferent
who'll entertain himself with my little songs.
And I think now I understand why,
and for whom I die.

THE BELLS OF ISLA NEGRA

I went to visit Pablo Neruda,
I was invited by "Ode to the Air."
And because the poet was somewhere far away,
only the tiny bell at the entranceway said to me:
"Salud, compañero!"

And so sitting at the table was the wind.
The setting consisted of two plates,
onion and green peppers.
Rotten angels were haunting it.
And sailing around in bottles
were strange vessels.

In the courtyard I met the celebrated bells.
They were hanging there like strung
Insurgents, fearfully prepared to rise up
as soon as a storm began anew.
I was sitting on the stone bench.
Gazing at the great black waves of the Pacific.
I kept quiet on the stone bench and felt myself
as fragile as the configuration of a cloud.

But as I left, I wrote across the sky:
"To Neruda. Wherever I may be,
once I hear the bells of Isla Negra,
I'll here."

IMAGE

Alongside the Pan-American Highway,
alongside this asphalt anaconda,
a girl – a Cholita – was offering,
raising up high, two bluish fish.
They were tied one above the other
like the two Americas. I would hardly
have remembered this face had not
the girl been so beautiful, the girl,
though a Cholita. I saw her in the morning
approaching the city of Caijete,
and in the evening I saw her again
leaving the city of Caijete. Offering,
raising up high, two blackish fish.
Aren't you tired out, Cholita girl?
Hasn't at least one lonely gringo stopped to
buy himself some excitement? No?
When I was drifting into my feverish sleep
later in the night, in Lima, there she stood
again the girl with two sharply pointed fish.
And many a night thereafter, kind
already in the other hemisphere,
I saw again the anaconda
and the wondrous girl, raising
up high two poison-tipped knives.

ADVENTURE
(A Madrigal)

Key and knife hold my room.
What ordinary words they are,
key and knife!

Why do I need the key?
I hardly know. I have no secrets,
I've no great fears.

Besides, behind lock and key
it only seems to me that we
should be together day and night.
(You know that love is my delight.)

I sharpen my lead pencils
with a knife. But I'm bound
to tell you, my dear comrades,
that the edge of my genealogical
strength is not at all blunted.

Knife and key
don't always meet
in one lair –
don't you agree?

But here, in returning
I find a folded knife
on a key holder.
I realize that you've left, my love.
I even understand our separation now.
What made you think of leaving
me this sign? Easy to read
yet dangerous as poppy seed.

You're the key. You patiently unlock
sweet truths and bitter truths.

I am the knife.
I'm the knife.
I cut these lines.

A CURSE ON COLUMBUS

Don Cristóbal Colón,
or Columbus, or whatever
you like to call yourself –
unlucky man, naive and
witless. There is no mercy
for you anymore! You transformed
our vision of the world. You
transformed the world itself.
History at once began to be the "New Age."
There is no excuse for you anymore!
Why didn't you listen to the
admiral on the golden mainland
when he urged you in a whisper:

"Listen, my dear fellow, listen!
You take on storms and unheard of spaces,
but don't ever forget me!
Because the most important thing
ultimately is me, with whom you took tea!

And so, the noblemen of Spain
are bored. It is said, Columbus,
that you're a crook. You sail off
to the West for the sheer joy of it.
And the route you've discovered
is not to India at all, the devil
knows where it's to. And besides,
instead of praying, you get drunk
and go whoring. Curse on you!
Curse you! Curse you!!

Surely you understand
what lies ahead of you?

Your continent will bear
a stranger's name.
And as for you —
whip and derision,
syphilis and ruin!

Don Cristóbal Colón,
why aren't you miserable?
Why don't you crawl on your knees?
Why are you hanging about
the harbor contentedly
with the leprous beggars?
You're searching for something.
A cloud? Or a ghost?
A medusa among the stars?

You really are a revolting man!
You're a monster! You can see
something after all! You can see
something we still cannot discern ourselves

AFTERLOVE

A long time ago I met
a young witch. A beauty
unsurpassed by others.
You were this beauty.
You gave me something to drink,
so I might remain forever faithful,
determined to be yours and yours only.

Remember how we played,
both of us, with kisses?
Remember how we played,
both of us, with love?
And by the time we understood
that these were true kisses,
and by the time we understood that this
was true love, the play, darling,
ended! Ended the play, darling!

And my arm returned to being
just an arm, and no longer a wing.
And the bed returned to being
only a bed. The heavens,
nothingness. But then what is it
that unites us now,
intoxicates us now,
consumes us now?
What is it called?
Answer! Perhaps afterlove?

I hear a single heart.
It beats fearfully and fiercely.
But we are both so close,
I do not know whether it is
my heart or yours, darling.

CHRISTMAS

Death arrived at Christmas —
half past two at night.
With a howl from the beyond
my dog, already marked by fate, greeted her.
I ran in, barefoot and sleepy, and I saw—
there they stood — black — He and She,
two darknesses with shining teeth.

Thirteen years earlier —
a red ribbon round his neck,
eyes barely open — the beast Fidelity
licked me as if making a vow.
In vain we named him Gaius
(not Caesar like every second dog.)
No one has managed to rebaptize his fate
even after a Regeneration Process.

We broke him of the habit of pissing in my shoes.
Generously we accustomed him to sharing our food.
(According to the Dominicans' rule —
dog must have what a master has!)

As it turned out, we had been eating poison
for so long! My Gaius had eaten up my dinner.
In vain we prayed — Forgive him, Death!
Because he knew what he was doing.
His legs died first
and down he fell.
He looked at me with his enormous
speaking eyes:
"Don't go away! Watch me to the end!..".—
And growled terribly. And bit again into
the darkness. By now he looked like
a heart that had been taken out
and was still pounding on the floor.

I sat beside him holding
his dying snout. The foam grew
cold and he stopped shivering.
Then it was time to open the door
to the balcony as the poet wished.

At nine the fog is thinning out.
The woodpecker is knocking on the
rotting poplar as if knocking up a coffin.

Gaius is lying wrapped up
in the kitchen table oil-cloth.
As if taken down from the cross.
Pieta! I and the woman artist are awkwardly
digging a grave. In this crooked world
we've hardly found a proper spade.
The ground is cracking up with roots.
I find a rusty key in the deep earth

and fling it upwards to unlock the heavens.
While the dog and Fidelity by a last,
great effort we thrust in this mud-caked
keyhole of the nothingness.

Out from the neighbors' houses,
out through hand-knitted curtains peek
the eyes of vigilance. Information shall
be sent that suspicious persons
are hiding a corpse or a treasure.
They'll dig it up. Damn! Let them! —
Since this is the fate of all pharaohs,
Caesars, leaders and knights of faithfulness. . .

Sleet is falling. Frozen tears
from the angels of dogs. And that it may
pile up and cover the grave
masked with branches like a wolf-pit.
I start philosophizing:
The wolf is the dog of the gods.
The wolf is a dog, true to its dead master.
Or maybe man is a god with a dead dog.

The holiday, with its radiant Christmas trees,
is over with its presents, its crafty forgiveness.
But even on Christmas Eve there comes an hour when
loners walk dogs under the undecorated branches.
Forgotten people give memories.
Oppressed people give Man
freedom from the global state.

And I am walking through the friendship grave-yard.
Walking only a dog's soul. It runs round excitedly.
It sniffs at the bushes. But there's no way
it can leave its sign. It runs back to me but it can't
lick me. And I don't know how to caress it. . .

An evening demonstration's coming from the square.
It's heading to the Television building and it's chanting:
"Down with the government!" "Down with the communists!"
"Death to the poets who write about dog's souls!"
Death! Death! Death!
Res, non verba!

SAINT VICTORY

Against my will,
something chooses me…

I have always been friend to hermits,
with the doomed, the condemned, etc.

Cognac and beer in the little restaurant
at the railway station—
Once they prospered—
they would forget me, and I them, of course.

Only you, Cezanne, are stubborn still.
You are a man of nasty fiber, Paul.
(I can't help it.)

And you keep painting,
painting until the final
ray of light. Victoire,
Sainte Victoire! Saint Victory!

This mountain,
why is it forever
in front of your eyes?
Why does it walk before you?
Won't it go away at last
to give way to another outline
or just make it possible to see
if there is anything beyond it?

Perhaps a road will speak out.
Perhaps a sacred river will begin to see.
Victoire, Sainte Victoire!
Saint Victory!

In the end everyone will
exclaim that you are a genius,
that all threads start from you.

But this is inconsequential.
Fame is not a good companion.
From now on words are a muddle…
Victoire, Sainte Victoire!
Saint Victory!

CAPRICE No. 18

To William Meredith: on his birthday

When you must speak, don't hold your tongue!
God gives and God will take away
speech, friendship, dignity;
gives — not voice, nor words, but speech.
William is nearly mute.
But we speak with one another.
We move neither lip nor hand.
But with his eyes alone
he tells me everything.
And I follow everything.
I fill our cups with old red everything.
And then the sunset is our toast.
There is no better way to talk.
Thus roofs will talk to darkening clouds.
There is no better way to talk.
Thus the clock beyond repair talks with night dreams.
Thus the dead will talk
with those preparing to live again,
preparing to wash away all their memories,
the way a knife is honed to strike again.
Thank you then for the talks, my friend.
I do not know
why I should be optimistic. But I am,
and so you will not feel alone.

ROOFS

To Bogomil Rainov

Grandfather's roof was made of slate
and weeds grew on its craggy shelf.
"Where is my grandfather's house?" I ask.
"It fell in ruins all by itself,"

they tell me. "Look how we've paved the yard."
And there is the old roof, stone by stone,
flagging the court. But I can't believe
that that strong old house collapsed on its own.

It was a beautifully fashioned house,
cozy, in human kindness furled,
but alas it had the same defects
as Grandfather's vision of the world.

The thick slate roof was terribly heavy
and the house itself had no foundations.
Very slowly it sank in the ground
with fate of all such houses and nations.

I'm sure that old house didn't fall to pieces
but slowly, slowly, of its own great weight
sank till the roof is level with the earth
and now I walk like a cat on its slate.

Box-trees rise from the flues like smoke
while down below the hearth burns fair,
the pot is boiling—nothing is changed
in Grandfather's lost Atlantis there.

And father, a little boy, is curled
in Grandmother's lap. His eyes are wide.
"Quick, go to sleep now, the bogey man
is on the roof." Father listens, terrified.

Yes! There is something there! He shudders
deliciously, and hearing proof
he falls asleep and dreams he dreams
my heavy footsteps on the roof.

It is cruelly hard to build a roof
that time's foundations can hold in place.
The superstructure (as Marx would say)
should never overload the base.
And those who write should think of things
as real as roof-trees, strong and straight.
Someone with lightning in his wings
has started walking on our slates.

THE DECEPTIVE PLAY OF THE SEASONS

(New London Quartet)

1. Spring Viola

A torrential spring wake-upper fell.
(O Lord, a new word loping in!)
Turned then to snow. And then storm.
A huge sea-tide forced back
the river's rushing power.
But couldn't push back time.
Cyclamens,
daffodils, survived.
Still, that day the tree of life
lost mighty branches.

I am standing now on the remains of the sun,
watching.
Merely watching.
In the park – graveyard
of the early settlers –
a half-full bottle, gleams.
A windowless ship has put up in the port.
It reminds me of something. Seems like a coffin!
A bird I cannot name flies past.
It calls the future with antediluvian cry.
Or else it is its wooden wings that creak.

I am listening.
Just listening.
I like such simple things.
The more primitive they are,
the more universal they seem to me.
And the Universe is composed of primal elements.
We alone are composed of generalities,
of formulae, of rules and of mortality.

2. Summer Violin

To be a future one... All right. But in that case
your eyes should read ahead for several bars,
which means to be not quite contemporary.

This transient, summer world of ours
is painted with transparent gouache;

the blank spaces, the rests, untouched
by brush or bow, prompt
different solutions. Too late now, however.

Sound has disappeared,
blossom withered.
On this virgin plane even tears
leave a scar, a crater formed
by a meteor.
An eye of Maldoror...

Fireflies no longer recognize me.
The moon lifts.
Nostalgia comes flooding in.
And the poppy fields within me grow wild.
And I am greeting even total strangers:
"Good evening! This
Is Ocean Avenue, am I right?"
I don't give a damn about the answers.

Scarcely do I touch reality. Like a flageolet.
And a distant mica South smolders
in the final line.

3. Autumn Cello

Now, I already dread the autumn—
my former love,
Mist invades the essence,
And I can't breathe in

the blues and greens. They come together
and fall apart in mystery.
I love them. But why do they conceal
something from me and my brother Cain?

Were we not freed from the same bonds?
Why should the color of our wounds be different
— like the eyes of angels
from the eyes of devils?

Nuances, from emerald to aquamarine —
ocean scents, scents of Port Mystic, of a hobo.
The ghost-ship will make its way through me
sweeping me away into the folk legend.

Are the palms of the maple there still stained with
blood from our separations and from the cross-road
junction curse? And are divinely scarlet tears still
rolling down the cheeks of Mount Perelick?

4. And Winter Clavichord

Earth may be for snow
what the skies, so ultimate, are for us.
This profound century is asking for its end. But now...
big snow is landing on Kennedy Airport.
No programs can accommodate it.
Deserted runways. Planes are deaf and dumb
like keys, unfingered by the superior,
this new and unexpected God of white.

We are sitting silently in lounges
under the darkened information screens
like implied messages
wordless overhead.

These are the transitory prisons
for our free will.

Soon the storm will fade away.
Flights will be resumed.
They'll give us back the cancelled space.
It's only freedom
that hates being liberated.
I noticed
how it broke through the lounge wall
and mingled with the storm.

I take advantage of the breakthrough
to throw my rhymes
into the stream of time,
of consciousness or mystery.
The way you throw the gun after a duel,
a love diary – after a break-up,
and the die after... Not before that

And there is no sign left in heaven.
Haughty snow
is landing on Kennedy Airport.

TRANSLATOR

Valentin Krustev

Valentin Krustev was born in Pazardzhik, Bulgaria, on April 26, 1949. Law graduate, he has worked mostly as a translator.

Valentin has translated extensively from and into English and from Russian, and has translated over fifty books of fiction and poetry by a number of authors, to name just a few: Alexander Taylor, Andrew Oerke, Jack Harte, Joseph Brodsky, Irwin Show, Richard Harteis, William Meredith, Bozhana Apostolova, Ekaterina Vitkova, Ekaterina Yossifova, Georgui Konstantinov, Lyubomir Levchev, Tanya Kolyovska, etc.

A book of his own poems titled *Between Heaven and Earth* was published by Orpheus Press, Sofia, in 2005. Some of his poems have been translated and published in literary magazines in Hungary, Russia and the USA.

ARTIST

Stoimen Stoilov

1944   Born in Varna (Bulgaria)
1972   Graduated from the Academy of Fine Arts in Sofia (Bulgaria).
Lives and works in Vienna (Austria) since 1991.

ONE-PERSON EXHIBITIONS IN:

Australia, Austria, Bulgaria, Canada, Czech Republic, France, Finland, Germany, Italy, Japan, Luxembourg, Norway, Russian Federation, Slovakia, Sweden, Switzerland, United States of America.

BIENNALES AND SALONS

Print Biennale, Varna (Bulgaria); Europ Art, Geneva (Switzerland); International Print Triennale, Chamallières (France); Biennale des artistes jurassiens, Delemont (Switzerland); Print Biennale, Ljubljana (Slovenia); Salon d'automne, Paris (France); Print Biennale, Fredrikstad (Norway); Print Biennale, Cracow (Poland); International Print Exhibition, Biella (Italy); Art Expo, New York (USA); Salon du dessin et de la peinture à l'eau, Paris (France); Print Biennale, Sao Paulo (Brazil); Biennale, Brno (Czech Republic); Biennale, Bratislava (Slovakia)

PRIZES

2009   The title Professor
1991   Gottfried von Herder Prize for his complete works, University of Vienna (Austria)
1991   Prize at the 2nd Print Triennale, Chamallières (France)

1985 Grand Prix for Bulgarian Participants at the 3rd Print Biennale, Varna (Bulgaria)
1984 Prize at Art Expo, New York (USA), granted by the foundation Bilan de l'art contemporain.
1983 The 'Iliya Petrov' Grand Prix for Mural Painting awarded by the Union of Bulgarian Artists, Sofia (Bulgaria)
1982 Silver Medal at the International Exhibition in Leipzig (Germany)
1976 Grand Prix of the Biennale, Brno (Czech Republic)

He has been awarded many other national prizes for print and drawing.

PRIVATE COLLECTIONS AND MUSEUMS

Austria
Museum of Graphic Art Albertina, Vienna
Vienna Ministry of Foreign Affairs, Vienna
Artothek, Vienna

Bulgaria
The National Art Gallery, Sofia
Municipal Museum of Art, Varna

France
Bibliothque nationale de France, Paris
Fonds national d'art contemporain, Paris
Art Dialogue Foundation, Paris

Germany
Museum of Art Villa Merkel, Esslingen
Museum of Graphic Art of the Schreiner Foundation, Bad Steben
Ludwig Forum, Aachen

Russia
Pushkin Museum of Art, Moscow

USA.
The Library of Congress, Washington DC
New York Public Library
Princeton University
Yale University
Florida State University (Strozier Library)
Florida Atlantic University (Jaffe Collection)
Middlebury College (Starr Library)

Works in private collections:
Austria, Australia, Bulgaria, France, Finland, Germany, Japan, Luxembourg, Norway, Sweden, and the United States of America.

ABOUT THE AUTHOR

Lyubomir Levchev

Lyubomir Levchev was born in Troyan, Bulgaria, on April 27, 1935 and is regarded as one of the great poets of Eastern Europe with international renown.

He has a long and distinguished history of commitment and service to literature and culture. He served as Chairman of the Bulgarian Writers' Union (1979-1988), First Deputy Secretary of Culture of Bulgaria, and Editor-in-Chief of the literary weekly of the Bulgarian Writers' Union, *Literaturen Front*.

He is a member of the European Academy of Science, Art, and Culture, and the European Academy of Poetry. His many international awards include: the Gold Medal for Poetry of the French Academy and the honorary title of 'Knight of Poetry' from the French Government (1985); the Medal of the Venezuela Writers' Association (1985); the Máté Zalka and Boris Polevoy awards, Russia (1986); the Grand Prize of the Alexander Pushkin Institute and the Sorbonne (1989); the Fernando Rielo World Prize for Mystical Poetry (1993); the Golden Wreath of the Struga Poetry Evenings, Macedonia (2010); the Bulgarian State Award Order of the Balkan Mountains 1st Class (2006).

Levchev is the founder and editor of the International Literary Magazine *Orpheus*. He has over thirty poetry books and three novels published in Bulgarian. The latest two among those are the autobiographical novel *Lament of the Dead Time* (2011) and the collection of selected and new poems *77 Poems* (2012). Over 58 of his books have been translated and published in 36 countries worldwide.